# A Multicultural Portrait of
# The Civil War

By Carol Ann Piggins

**Marshall Cavendish**
New York • London • Toronto

**Cover:** Shackled hands symbolize slavery in this detail from a mosaic.

Published by
**Marshall Cavendish Corporation**
2415 Jerusalem Avenue
P.O. Box 587
North Bellmore, New York 11710, USA

© Marshall Cavendish Corporation, 1994

Edited, designed, and produced by Water Buffalo Books, Milwaukee

Project director: Mark Sachner
Art director: Sabine Beaupré
Picture researcher: Diane Laska
Editor: David Wright
Indexer: Valerie Weber
Marshall Cavendish development editor: MaryLee Knowlton
Marshall Cavendish editorial director: Evelyn Fazio

Editorial consultants: Mark S. Guardalabene, Milwaukee Public Schools; Yolanda Ayubi, Ph.D., Consultant on Ethnic Issues, U.S. Department of Labor

For their help in the preparation of this book, the editors would like to thank Kirsty P. Collins, Kristi Ludwig, and Petra Press.

**Picture Credits:** © H. Abernathy/H. Armstrong Roberts: Cover, 22; © Archive Photos: 26, 28 (top), 29; Sabine Beaupré, 1993: 8; © The Bettmann Archive: 6-7, 9, 10, 11, 14, 17, 18, 19, 20, 21, 24, 25 (both), 27, 32 (both), 33 (both), 34, 35, 37 (left), 38, 41, 42, 44, 45 (both), 47, 48 (both), 50, 51, 54, 55, 56, 58, 60-61, 62 (both), 63, 64 (both), 65 (top), 67, 68 (both), 69, 70, 71, 72, 73; © Culver Pictures: 28 (bottom); © H. Armstrong Roberts: 15 (both), 36, 37 (right), 39, 46, 65 (bottom); © Sipley/H. Armstrong Roberts: 30; © UPI/Bettmann: 74, 75

**Library of Congress Cataloging-in-Publication Data**

Piggins, Carol Ann.
    A multicultural portrait of the Civil War / Carol Ann Piggins.
       p. cm. — (Perspectives)
    Includes bibliographical references and index.
    Summary: Portrays the Civil War from the vantage point of Afro-Americans and women.
    ISBN 1-85435-660-7 :
    1. United States—History—Civil War, 1861-1865—Afro-Americans—Juvenile literature. 2. United States—History—Civil War, 1861-1865—Social aspects—Juvenile literature. 3. Afro-Americans—History—To 1863—Juvenile literature. 4. Afro-Americans—History—1863-1877—Juvenile literature. 5. Minorities—United States—History—19th century—Juvenile literature. 6. Pluralism (Social sciences)—United States—History—19th century—Juvenile literature. [1. United States—History—Civil War, 1861-1865. 2. Afro-Americans—History—To 1863. 3. Afro-Americans—History—1863-1877. 4. Minorities.] I. Title. II. Series: Perspectives (Marshall Cavendish Corporation)
E540.N3P54   1993
973'.0496073—dc20
                                                               93-10319
                                                                 CIP
                                                                 AC

To PS – MS

Printed and bound in the U.S.A.

# CONTENTS

## About *Perspectives*

*Perspectives* is a series of multicultural portraits of events and topics in U.S. history. Each volume examines these events and topics not only from the perspective of the white European-Americans who make up the majority of the U.S. population, but also from that of the nation's many people of color and other ethnic minorities, such as African-Americans, Asian-Americans, Hispanic-Americans, and American Indians. These people, along with women, have been given little attention in traditional accounts of U.S. history. And yet their impact on historical events has been great.

The terms *American Indian*, *Hispanic-American*, *Anglo-American*, *Black*, *African-American*, and *Asian-American*, like *European-American* and *white*, are used by the authors in this series to identify people of various national origins. Labeling people is a serious business, and what we call a group depends on many things. For example, a few decades ago it was considered acceptable to use the words *colored* or *Negro* to label people of African origin. Today, these words are outdated and often a sign of ignorance or outright prejudice. Some people even consider *Black* less acceptable than *African-American* because it focuses on a person's skin color rather than national origins. And yet *Black* has many practical uses, particularly to describe people whose origins are not only African but Caribbean or Latin American as well.

If we must label people, it's better to be as specific as possible. That is a goal of *Perspectives* — to be as precise and fair as possible in the labeling of people by race, ethnicity, national origin, or other factors, such as gender or disability. When necessary and possible, Americans of Mexican origin will be called *Mexican-Americans*. Americans of Irish origin will be called *Irish-Americans*, and so on. The same goes for American Indians: when possible, specific Indians are identified by their tribal names, such as the *Chippewa* or *Mohawk*. But in a discussion of various Indian groups, tribal origins may not always be entirely clear, and so it may be more practical to use *American Indian*, a term that has widespread use among Indians and non-Indians alike.

Even within a group, individuals may disagree over the labels they prefer for their group: *Black* or *African-American*? *Hispanic* or *Latino*? *American Indian* or *native American*? *White*, *Anglo*, or *European-American*? Different situations often call for different labels. The labels used in *Perspectives* represent an attempt to be fair, accurate, and perhaps most importantly, to be mindful of what people choose to call *themselves*.

# A Note About *The Civil War*

The American Civil War lasted four years — less time than the American Revolution or the Vietnam War, and about as long as World War II or the Korean Conflict. And yet, like no other series of battles in the nation's history, it affected the United States on a number of fronts, not the least of which were the critical issue of slavery and the question of whether the Union would stay intact at a very young and tender stage of its growth. As this book will show, the war was fought on a personal level as well as a political or military level, affecting people in ways that can still be measured today:

**African-Americans,** brought to this country against their will and forced to live in a strange, hostile culture. The war told them that, despite almost 250 years of suffering in America, there was hope.

**White southerners,** whose dreams of controlling their land and their way of life were dashed by defeat.

**Native Americans,** who saw their land cultivated and themselves displaced as Europeans continued to settle the country.

**Political figures,** who gambled that people cared enough to fight to keep the young nation whole and to support a strong central government.

**Immigrants,** who came to the U.S. in much greater numbers after 1850 than before. These people, from Russia's plains, China's rice paddies, and Bavaria's forests, found themselves viewing — and sometimes playing a part in — a conflict they knew little about.

**People struggling under colonial oppression** throughout the Americas. Among the most interested observers were other European colonists in the western hemisphere, such as the Portuguese who settled Brazil. They finally freed their African slaves in 1888.

Americans realized in the wake of the war that the North did not so much beat the South as outproduce it. The conflict proved that a military power had to be an industrial power. It also had lasting social effects: the South saw itself and was seen by others as different from the rest of the nation. Prejudice became a two-way street as southern whites continued to dislike Blacks and people who sympathized with Blacks, while northerners looked down on their countrymen from Dixie.

These and other deeply embedded factors, some predating the war, along with other feelings spawned by the war and passed from one generation to the next, still affect the way people in the United States live with and feel about one another. The fact is that more than one hundred years since slavery was officially abolished in the U.S., its citizens have been unable to shake free from their preoccupation with the issue of race — despite the continuing waves of new immigrants who do not carry with them memories of an American war to free people from slavery.

Harriet Tubman (far left) poses with a group of slaves she helped escape.

# CHAPTER ONE

# The Seeds of Civil War

Harriet Tubman was six years old in 1827. The child lived with her mother, father, and nine sisters and brothers in a one-room log cabin. The floor was hard-packed earth, and wind whistled through cracks between the logs. The tiny girl's chores included carrying heavy water buckets to field hands. Harriet would some day leave the South to become a leader of her people. But in Dorchester County, Maryland, and throughout the southern United States, Harriet and Black children like her had little time to play or hope or dream. Harriet Tubman was a slave.

Before Harriet turned seven, Mr. Brodas, her owner, took her from her family by hiring her out to a neighbor. Harriet didn't want to leave, and her parents begged Brodas not to take the little girl away, but they could not stop him. They were the property of Brodas, who could do as he pleased.

## Slavery Splits the Nation

Such scenes were played out again and again in America's slave states before the Civil War: families were broken up and never reunited; young children were hired out to neighboring farmers or sold to plantation owners in other states; husbands were sold from wives; mothers were sold from children.

As stories spread in the North about the mistreatment and the families torn apart, more and more northerners grew to despise slavery. Abolitionists — people whose goal was to wipe out slavery — gave speeches and distributed pamphlets to rally opposition to slavery. Some northerners thought force should be used to break up slavery. The issue eventually divided the young nation.

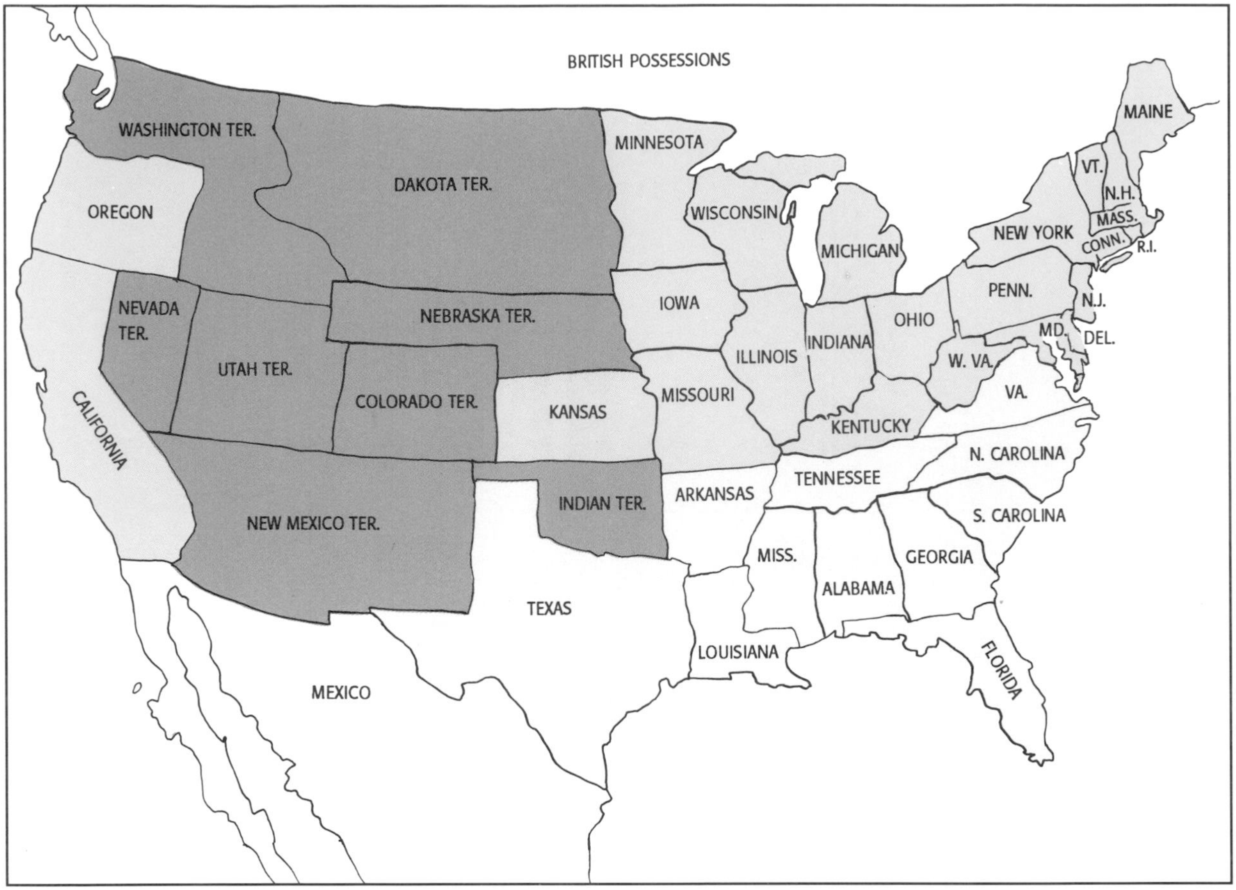
BRITISH POSSESSIONS
WASHINGTON TER.
OREGON
DAKOTA TER.
MINNESOTA
MAINE
VT.
N.H.
MASS.
CONN.
R.I.
NEW YORK
WISCONSIN
MICHIGAN
IOWA
NEBRASKA TER.
NEVADA TER.
UTAH TER.
COLORADO TER.
CALIFORNIA
KANSAS
MISSOURI
ILLINOIS
INDIANA
OHIO
PENN.
N.J.
MD.
DEL.
W. VA.
VA.
KENTUCKY
N. CAROLINA
TENNESSEE
ARKANSAS
INDIAN TER.
NEW MEXICO TER.
S. CAROLINA
MISS.
GEORGIA
ALABAMA
TEXAS
LOUISIANA
FLORIDA
MEXICO

By 1861, the U.S. had thirty-four states and several territories. Eleven states would secede from the Union to form the Confederate States of America. The part of Virginia known as "West Virginia" rejected secession and was admitted into the Union as a state in 1863.

Seeds of the Civil War were sown when the first slave was brought to America in 1619. Other issues intensified the problem, and by the mid-1800s, battle loomed.

By the outbreak of the Civil War in 1861, the United States would be made up of thirty-four states, eleven of which would eventually vote to become part of the Confederate States of America. The outnumbered South worried about losing power in Congress. As new territories west of the Mississippi River were settled, southerners tried to keep them open to slavery. This would give the South more votes in Washington when the territories became states. Northerners wanted the territories to be free. Consequently, politics and power struggles added to tensions, which were already quite high. Southerners also felt that a state should control its own destiny — that it had the right to leave the United States.

Social differences also drove a wedge between North and South. While the North became industrialized, the South maintained an old-fashioned plantation economy. European-American southerners needed slaves to run plantations, yet they spoke of slavery as their burden. They believed plantation life was good for slaves, guaranteeing employment, medical care, and a minimum standard of living into old age. Rather than evil, the system brought Christianity and a higher standard of living to the slaves — whom they claimed to have rescued from primitive Africa. Throughout its young life, the U.S. had demonstrated that

European-Americans in the North as well as in the South could accept slavery as a part of American life. Yet most people in the North — and many northerners held racist attitudes of their own toward African-Americans — disagreed with such contrived arguments to justify slavery.

## The Making of a Slave

By 1857, southern slavery had existed for more than two centuries and was inseparable from the region's life and economy. Slavery provided most of the labor for the production of cotton, corn, and tobacco. Nearly 400,000 European-American men owned 4 million slaves at a total worth of 2 billion dollars.

Although some owners cared for their slaves well — usually as a way of protecting their investment — many treated them like livestock. Slaves worked from sunrise to sunset, spending long hours in the hot sun with no rest. They performed endless, backbreaking labor, with overseers using whips and dogs to force them on.

In the South, slaves were raised to believe that slavery was their rightful position. They were born into slavery and the plantation system was designed to keep them enslaved. Owners tried to convince slaves they were helpless, dominating them physically. In addition to other hardships and humiliations, slave women often were forced to perform sexual acts for their owners.

When slaves disobeyed, talked back, or made mistakes, they were whipped or beaten. They could suffer if the slaveowner was in a bad mood or wanted to show off for friends, family, or other slaves. Plantation owners and overseers often carried guns and threatened even greater violence to slaves who failed to do their jobs. Slaves had no weapons and few material goods. They were, in fact, forbidden to own not only guns but even drums! Slaveowners worried that potentially

### Harriet Tubman and the Underground Railroad

From the time Harriet Tubman escaped from slavery in 1849 until the beginning of the Civil War, she made eighteen trips to help slaves flee to free states or to Canada on the Underground Railroad. She aided about three hundred slaves, including her parents.

She was perhaps the most famous of the Underground Railroad leaders, and African-Americans of her day called her Moses, after the man who led the Jews out of slavery in Biblical Egypt. At one time, rewards for her capture totaled forty thousand dollars. Tubman used desperate measures when necessary. Pursued by slavecatchers, she once urged her weary companions on by threatening them with a loaded revolver!

A friend of fellow abolitionists Ralph Waldo Emerson and John Brown, she was deeply religious and deeply committed. During the war, Tubman served as a nurse, scout, and spy for the Union Army in South Carolina. She helped free more than 750 slaves during one military campaign. Tubman stands in the forefront of a long line of strong, smart, and ingenious workers for the Underground Railroad.

Old slaves in the cotton fields.

rebellious slaves on neighboring plantations might use tom-toms or similar devices to communicate with one another.

Slaves were taunted and belittled. Names given them were often meant as sarcastic jokes. A slave might be called Nero, Plato, Caesar, or Prince, for example, after some famous or powerful figure in history, in contrast to his powerless state. Slaves might have no name at all, being referred to only as "boy" or "girl." Ways to keep slaves in their place were outlined in magazines such as *Southern Cultivator*, *Farmers' Register*, *Carolina Planter*, and *South-Western Farmer*.

Rights and privileges that were given to European-Americans were unknown. Slaves had no books or schools. They could not legally meet unless a white adult was present. Written passes or a white escort were needed to travel or to leave the plantation. Slaves could not decide what kind of work to do or where to live. Local patrols made surprise visits to slave quarters to break up secret meetings or to search for runaway slaves.

This lack of control over their lives was a strong dehumanizing force, but slaves faced other hardships. Though family ties were not honored, owners encouraged slaves to have children because it increased the owners' wealth. In this and many other ways, masters thought of slaves as property. Just as they bred and sold horses, sheep, or cattle when they needed money, they sold slaves. Even very young children could be sold away from their parents, often to a place so far away it was unlikely the family would ever be reunited.

While some slaves, especially those living in southern cities, could move about more freely than others and in some cases even accumulate money by doing work for cash, the vast majority of slaves depended completely on their masters for food, clothing, and shelter. Those needs were often met in substandard ways. Forced to live in inferior housing, most slaves were crowded into crude shacks. One Mississippi planter built twenty-four one-room huts, each measuring sixteen by fourteen feet, for 150 slaves. Rations were distributed weekly, and slaves were badly fed. A typical week of food for an adult was a peck (about eight quarts) of cornmeal and three to four pounds of salt pork. Sweet potatoes, peas, rice, syrup, and fruit were occasional luxuries.

Clothing was made of material so rough it scratched the skin. Many slaves went barefoot, partly because their shoes fit poorly and caused pain. Others received no shoes at all. In 1835, Congressman T.T. Bouldin of Virginia charged that "Many negroes had died from exposure as a consequence of flimsy fabric that will turn [away] neither wind nor weather."

Slaves tried to escape their harsh lives; some succeeded. Harriet Tubman escaped to Philadelphia as an adult. She devoted the rest of her life to helping others escape. But fleeing was difficult and dangerous. Whites on horseback patrolled the countryside looking for runaway slaves or for Blacks meeting illegally. When they found slaves without written passes, the well-armed white men captured and beat them. Slaves were returned to their plantations, where they could be beaten again.

Archie Booker, a former slave, describes the dangers of unescorted travel this way: "Yes, they had church meetings. People used to go from house to house. Old Harry Brown, he was a kind of preacher. He used to preach to us right smart. 'Cause they had to watch for the paddyrollers [patrollers]. They generally come in twos and threes. They come twixt eight and twelve at night. If they catch you having meetings, they'd arrest you. Yes sir! They had bloodhounds with them. 'Twarn't no way in the world you could get away. No sir! They didn't have the same men on the patrols all the time. Different men every night."

## The Slave Trade

One of the most powerful forces in the making of a slave was the slave trade itself. Dehumanizing from start to finish, the traffic in human lives was at best terrible and at worst fatal. Some historians estimate that from 1619, when the first Africans were brought to America, until 1808, when legal slave importation ended, over 1 million African men, women, and children were brought to the United States.

A slave auction.

There was no lack of people eager to profit from human misery. African tribes sometimes enslaved other Africans, usually prisoners of war, and often sold them to slave traders. Roving outlaws kidnapped hunters or others who became separated from their people. European slavers often ventured into the interior to capture Africans. Slave traders could be African, Arab, or European, and their trade extended throughout the Americas, including the Caribbean islands. Though cargo bound for North America was sent to the southern U.S., slave ships were often owned by New England merchants and financed by bankers in Boston, New York, and Philadelphia. Estimates of slaves imported into all of the Americas during the trans-Atlantic slave era are 10-15 million.

Captured Africans were stripped and forced to march for days to their continent's west coast, where ships waited to take them to America. Chained together and exposed to the relentless tropical sun, the captives grew weak and sick. Historians estimate that two out of every five captives fell prey to disease or weather or beatings and died before reaching the boats. Sometimes it took weeks to capture enough Africans to fill the ships, which often cruised from one port to another along the coast, picking up human cargo at each stop.

Those who made it to the coast were thrown into cages with other captives and then, once on board the ship, crowded into a dark hold for the passage to America. They were chained to a railing that ran the length of the ship, and unable to shift positions, they were forced to lie in their own blood and body wastes. Once a day, they were allowed above deck. There, they were forced to hop about so potential buyers wouldn't think they were too stiff to work.

Food on board was a daily handful of beans or rice cooked with yams and a drink of water from a cask. The passage to America usually took twenty-five to thirty-five days. Despite the brutality on board, many heroically resisted their fate and planted seeds of resistance that would flourish when the captives became slaves in America. Some mutinied against the ship's captain, and some even threw themselves overboard rather than face a life of bondage. As many as one-third of the captives died before the boat reached shore. The total loss of Africa's population to the slave trade, including both those who survived and those who died during the horrific Atlantic passage, is put at a staggering 20-30 million.

Once in America, the people were oiled to make their skins glisten. Open sores were hidden from potential buyers with blobs of tar. A bit of clothing made them presentable for sale. Buyers pushed and prodded, looking for defects. Slaves were given dental checks and paraded about to demonstrate their agility and strength. The owners of large plantations with cash in hand had first choice. Smaller farmers took what was left, making a down payment and paying the rest at harvest.

## The Southern Economy

The slave trade flourished because the plantation system depended on slavery. A plantation was a large agricultural operation with one main crop, usually cotton or tobacco. The operation was run by one man, perhaps with his sons, and an overseer with anywhere from twenty to five hundred slaves. Plantations needed many workers, and slave labor came cheap.

The South lent itself to a plantation economy because the soil was rich and the growing season long. A man could become wealthy growing a single crop on hundreds of acres, keeping the land under constant cultivation. Few people knew that planting the same crop year after year robbed the soil of important nutrients. One-crop farming contributed to the downfall of the Old South, dooming the plantation system even before the Civil War began.

Until the Civil War, planters — plantation owners — were in power in the South, even though only one southern white man in ten owned slaves. While some owned as many as five hundred slaves, half of the slaveowners held fewer than five. Many whites were poor, but they dreamed of becoming planters and owning slaves. And while the plantation system may have had its critics, especially in the North, the plantation itself was the widespread symbol of the South during the first half of the nineteenth century. Therefore, European-American southerners supported slavery.

Many southerners resented the North. They felt that the colonies would never have won their independence without the plantation wealth of Georgia, Virginia, and the Carolinas. Yet the North denied southern states power and respect. Southerners disliked the protective tariffs, or taxes, that northerners placed on clothing imported from Europe but made of southern cotton. Southerners were pressured into buying northern-made clothing if they wanted to buy at lower prices.

On the eve of the Civil War, the North controlled the nation's transportation and its industrial production. The North had 85 percent of the factories, 81 percent of the nation's bank deposits, 97 percent of the firearms, 72 percent of the railroad tracks, and 96 percent of all railroad equipment.

Southerners wanted to hold to traditional ways. There had been no technological innovation in the South beyond the invention of the cotton gin, a device that mechanically separated cotton from cotton seeds. There were few artists or craftsworkers. Middle-class businessmen, office workers, and skilled workers were almost nonexistent. People were either part of the plantation aristocracy or they were poor. Southerners wanted the federal government to leave their states alone.

It would be incorrect to say that the Civil War was fought solely to free the slaves. Politics and power were the reasons for the conflict. Businessmen and industrialists from the North were looking for ways to extend their interests into the rural South. Southerners felt that northern politicians were trying to run their lives through federal laws passed in Washington. Yet southern leaders themselves were to blame, too. They engaged in years of race baiting and telling friends and neighbors horror stories about northern control of southern lives. Such stories usually had racial themes, stirring white people's fears of losing a way of life that included slave labor.

The South had only about half the population of the North and had not yet been visited by the Industrial Revolution. Free public schools were the exception rather than the rule. Only half as many white children in the South attended school as in the North, and only about half the white population in the South could read or write before the Civil War. Among slaves, just one person in ten could read. Up north, the literacy rate among whites was 95 percent.

As land became more expensive, small planters suffered. They could not afford to buy land as their families grew. Young men had difficulty saving money. Poor whites who were not planters suffered more. Because of slavery, they couldn't get work on plantations, and there were few industrial jobs. A plantation owner would not pay a white laborer to work when he could get slave labor nearly free. Many poor whites became patrollers, guarding plantations to prevent slaves from running away. A white seeking employment might work as an overseer. These people hated slaves, blaming them for their own economic difficulties.

A slave gives a Christmas gift to the master and his wife.

## Plantation Life

**The Plantation Owner.** Plantation owners lived in what was called the big house. Some plantations — and their big houses — were much bigger than others. Regardless of size, they symbolized a way of life. This life was ruled by a code telling how women were to be treated, how a gentleman should speak, and how an argument should be settled. Honor was all-important. Around 1860, the idea of honor included an inner feeling of self-worth, refined manners, a good reputation, defense of family and country, and conforming to community wishes. Honor was even more important than making money. A plantation owner's status, and the respect he commanded from others, depended upon how clearly he lived by the code.

On a large plantation, the master or man of the house employed an overseer. This employee directed day-to-day activities of the slaves. The master met with the overseer to discuss work or problems but generally did not run the plantation himself. On a smaller plantation, the owner not only directed the work, he might labor in the fields along with his slaves. Servants in the big house cooked, cleaned, waited tables, and helped the master dress. That left time for the master to read, discuss politics, socialize with other plantation owners, and enjoy his family.

**Plantation Children.** The plantation owner's children had lives that in some ways mirrored those of their parents. Some children had their own servants. In many cases, they were cared for by a female slave. White children sometimes played with the slave children, but everyone understood that the white children were in charge.

The plantation owner's children were well clothed and well fed. They were entertained at parties and they visited other plantations with their parents. Many children had their own ponies and other pets. Tutors were often hired for reading, writing, and arithmetic, with a special room serving as the school. If the children attended school off the plantation, they rode to and from the school accompanied by a young slave who had to walk, carrying books.

### A childhood memory

Amalia Thompson Watts, a slaveowner's daughter, once reminisced about her childhood:

"One of the negro boys had found a dead chicken and we arranged for a great funeral. The boys made a wagon of fig branches, and four of them as horses. We tied a bow of black ribbon around the chicken's neck, and covered him with a white rag, and then marched in a procession singing one of the quaint negro hymns, all the white children next to the hearses, marching two by two, and the colored children following in the same order. . . .

"After marching all the way up the avenue and down again, we stopped at the grave, under the big magnolia tree by the gate, and my sister Maria preached a sermon from the text, 'We must all die,' and the chicken was buried with great solemnity."

## Slave Life

### A Life Based on Forced Labor.

The lives of plantation slaves were neither predictable nor pleasant. They knew they would work hard, of course. But the nature and location of the work were left to the plantation owner and his overseer. A slave could be assigned any task or be hired out to a neighbor. Most slaves lived in slave quarters some distance from the big house. On large plantations, the rows of cabins were arranged like houses on a street. The houses could be as comfortable as those of poor whites in the area. More often, they were shacks.

Slave cabins usually had only a single room, so all family activities, including sleeping, occurred there. Some cabins had no bedframes or other furniture, forcing slaves to sleep on beds of rags and straw. There were no blankets. When the dirt floors got wet, everyone's feet slid in the mud. As one slave recalled, "The damp earth soaked in the moisture till the floor was miry as a pig-sty."

Field hands labored from sunup until sundown. They planted, weeded, hoed, and chopped. Picking cotton was an especially

*Top and bottom:* Two post-Civil War scenes reminiscent of an era that is not so far in the past — slavery in the South.

difficult and painful task. The thorny casings that held the cotton cut the slaves' fingers. The field hands walked rows of cotton bent over, trailing long bags filled with their harvest.

House slaves often lived in their master's home. They worked fewer hours, but they could be called by the master at any moment. Slave children who cared for the master's babies slept on the floor of the infants' rooms. Slaves too old to work might be given small patches of garden to tend for themselves. Everybody — slave and master alike — ate food grown by forced labor in large vegetable gardens.

**Slave Children.** Slave children lived much like their parents. As soon as they were old enough to be of service, they worked. They might work in the field or in the big house. They might fan a hot master, watch younger children, hold yarn

## Free Blacks

In 1860, there were 488,070 free Blacks in the United States. This was 11 percent of the Black population. A little more than half, 250,787, lived in the South. Some were indentured servants who had completed their terms of service. Others gained liberty through military service. Most had been given their freedom by former masters, either because of a blood relationship or because the slave had served faithfully and obediently. In some cases, masters simply lost faith in slavery.

In addition, there were some African-Americans who purchased their own freedom. They usually had a skill or trade and accumulated money by hiring themselves out. Often they lived in towns, where being hired came more easily. Many were carpenters, tailors, or apothecaries. Some were farmers, and, in the South, some even owned slaves! In 1860, in Virginia, 157 African-Americans owned real estate and free Blacks worked in fifty-four different kinds of jobs.

Nevertheless, free Blacks faced restrictions. They had to carry a certificate of freedom or face being jailed, hired out, or sold. They had to observe curfew and were denied the right of assembly. They could gather only for church.

Conditions were better in the North. Blacks were able to support each other through newspapers, conventions, fraternal organizations, and political and reform movements. Blacks in New York City in 1856 owned $200,000 in bank deposits. Cincinnati Blacks in 1852 owned property worth more than $500,000.

But things were not perfect. Free Blacks could vote without condition in only four states — Massachusetts, Maine, New Hampshire, and Vermont. In New York, an African-American could not vote unless he owned $250 in real estate. Indiana's 1851 constitution barred Blacks from entering the state, and Illinois required them to post a bond of $1,000 as a guarantee of good conduct.

as the lady of the house spun, shovel in the stable, or perform other tasks. Slave children received no formal education and had more or less time to play depending on the wishes of their master.

Very young children were supervised by Black women too old to work the fields. These small children still had some time to play. They explored neighboring woods. They played marbles. Sadly, some reenacted slave trading and the beating of belligerent slaves.

Few slave children were fed on plates at tables. Instead, they ate from long troughs, like animals. Food was dumped, the children were called, and they knelt to get what food they could with their hands and mouths. All slave children ate from the same trough. No one could afford to be polite or civilized.

### Off the Plantation

While the plantation system dominated the economy and the image of the South, not everyone lived within that system. A very small number of slaves were set free by their masters, and many southerners farmed without the benefit of hundreds of slaves.

Many southerners also lived in cities and small towns, many as small as Belmont, Missouri, which had only three houses. Regardless of how or where anyone lived and worked in the antebellum (prewar) South, most European-Americans held common racist attitudes toward Blacks and subscribed to the same beliefs and values. Plantation society was the admired style of life, slaveholding was acceptable—even a duty—and the North was increasingly evil.

### The North Diversifies

In the North, there was no similar common purpose or identity to compare with plantation life. While the South remained firmly rooted in an agricultural way of life, the increasingly urban North relied less on farming as an economic and social base. In 1860, the South had only three cities with populations of 40,000 or more: New Orleans had 165,000, and Richmond and Charleston had 40,000 each. The North had at least a dozen cities with populations of more than 40,000. Topping the list were New York with 800,000 people, Philadelphia with 565,000, and Boston with 165,000. Chicago had grown from 250 in 1800 to 100,000 in

1860. In the North, slavery would have been less profitable in rural areas than in the South. The growing season was shorter, so farmers did not have year-round field work. The North's economic activity centered on small farms and on industries rather than on huge plantations.

**Northern Farm Life.** A northern farmer usually worked the land with his sons and a hired hand or two. Work was hard, but most farmers owned the land they tilled. Women cooked, canned, made butter and cheese, and tended chickens. Everybody in the family enjoyed the benefits of each other's labor.

By the time of the Civil War, several northern states had laws guaranteeing an education for all children. In rural communities, teachers lived with farm families. Women teachers could not marry, smoke, or swear, and students sat on hard benches, writing on slates instead of paper. Schools usually were one-room wooden buildings built by neighbors.

**Business Life.** Northern business and industry were on the rise. Many people who lived and worked in cities had nothing to do with farming other than eating what the farmer produced. In contrast to settlers out west who were totally independent, city dwellers depended on each other. The person who made clothing all day bought food from someone else, just as the baker did not make his or her clothes. Money became increasingly important for trade.

A businessperson might work in a bank or a trading company or run a large industry. There were shops of every kind, shipbuilding yards, law offices, and publishing houses. New inventions, such as the railroad, gave rise to new businesses. Growth and change were everywhere.

Businessmen dressed in suits, rode in carriages, and lived in comfortable homes. The more affluent hired servants to cook, clean, and perform other household duties. Their children generally went to grade school, high school, and even college. Children had leisure time to read, play in parks, and daydream.

**Factory Life.** Life for factory workers was less pleasant. Many labored in sweatshops, putting in twelve- to fifteen-hour days producing textiles. The factories were crowded, dirty, and dangerous. Workers had to stand for long hours without a break and often had to lift heavy loads.

In 1832, two-fifths of all people employed in New England factories were ages seven to seventeen. They never worked less than ten hours, seldom less than twelve, and often fifteen or more. Entire families were hired to work for a group wage.

The first child labor law was passed in 1836. It stated that no child under fifteen could be

A mill in Fall River, Massachusetts. Child labor was common in the textile industry.

employed unless he or she had attended school at least three months in the preceding year. In 1842, Massachusetts limited child labor under twelve in textile factories to ten hours per day. Connecticut forbade employment of children under fourteen for more than ten hours a day in cotton or woolen mills. In 1848, Pennsylvania prohibited employment in textile mills of children under twelve. But laws were poorly enforced; they certainly were inadequate by today's standards. Children worked in almost every kind of factory, doing metalwork and making goods such as hats, cardboard boxes, and furniture.

Nineteenth-century factory workers often lived in crowded, dirty, rat-infested tenements. There was no central heat, and cooking was done on charcoal braziers. The workers made meager salaries. In Lowell, Massachusetts, farm girls were recruited to work in the cotton mills. They were paid $4 per week, $2.75 of which went for room and board. Factory workers rented rather than owned their dwellings.

## The Immigration Boom and an Appetite for Land

In 1780, more than three of four immigrants to the original thirteen United States were descendants of English and Irish settlers. Others were from Germany, the Netherlands, France, and Switzerland. Spain had been in the Southwest since the 1500s. Around 1850, Chinese laborers came to California to mine gold and work on the railroad.

The mid-1800s saw an immigration boom. From 1790 to 1840, fewer than a million immigrants arrived. But between 1841 and 1860, more than four million

An immigrant family arrives on Ellis Island.

immigrants landed, primarily from Ireland, Germany, Britain, and France. They were driven by famine due to bad harvests and by political revolution. Most arrived in the North to join relatives in large cities or on farms. Just prior to the Civil War, 71 percent of the nation's population lived in the North.

The appetite for land grew. As more and more land was taken in the East, settlers moved west, pushing out the American Indians who were already there.

## Settling the Land

In 1861, at the outbreak of the Civil War, there were thirty-four states and several territories still to be settled. Settlers who moved into the territories farmed, too, but only after a struggle to prepare the land. Their backbreaking labor included chopping down trees, removing stumps, hauling boulders, and building log cabins.

The farther settlers traveled from organized states, the more dangers they encountered. Trails were muddy and hazardous, and storms made passage difficult. Travelers lost their way and died on the journey. Life was rough and tumble, with outlaws as likely to travel west as families looking to make new homes.

Everyone in the family, including children, worked hard to make a new life in unfamiliar territory. Women labored alongside men clearing land and tending animals as well as cooking, gardening, and caring for children. There were no stores, no schools, and no churches. Everything was from scratch, with the family meeting its own needs. Money, at least in the early days, was of less use than hard work.

### Indians Lose Their Lands

The European attitude toward land differed from that of American Indians. Europeans believed land should be privately owned for the purpose of being exploited, while Indians believed the land could not be owned but should be used respectfully for the benefit of the tribe. Europeans wanted to cut trees for farm houses and to clear land. Indians wanted to use the land as they had for thousands of years — to hunt, fish, and gather nuts and berries. Europeans failed to understand or appreciate the highly developed cultures of the Indians they met. Though American Indians often tried to live in harmony with the new settlers, they became angry and sometimes fought back as they continually lost land.

As early in the history of the United States as 1787, the Northwest Ordinance stated that native "lands and property shall never be taken from them without their consent." But neither words nor treaties prevented land speculators and settlers from pouring into Ohio before it had been bought from the tribes. Nor did it stop settlers from moving westward for years to come.

While American Indians such as the Seminole in Florida harbored runaway slaves, others owned and operated slave plantations. The Cherokee and the

A Sioux Council.

Creek even started plantations as a way to protect their land. The attempt was futile: European-Americans seized Indian plantations when the Indians were removed west of the Mississippi in the 1830s.

The experience of American Indians frequently was little better than that of African-American slaves. In 1838, for example, sixteen thousand Cherokee were herded from Florida to Indian Territory (present-day Oklahoma) along what is known as the "Trail of Tears." Four thousand Indians died on that forced march. Though Indians were assured protection by the U.S. Supreme Court, President Andrew Jackson defied the Court in the 1830s by pushing the Indians west.

## Removal and Reservations

The government eventually moved most tribes in the eastern United States to the Indian Territory west of the Mississippi. At its peak size, around 1850, the Indian Territory extended from the Red River to the Missouri and from the state lines of Arkansas, Missouri, and Iowa to the 100th meridian.

The sad experience of Wisconsin tribes shows how Indians attempted to sidestep government policy. Several tribes were scheduled for removal as European-American settlement pushed westward, so the government met with them in Prairie du Chien, Wisconsin, in 1825, under pretext of keeping the peace. But the government really wanted the tribes to agree on boundaries so it could sell their land more easily. By 1848, the year Wisconsin became a state, all tribal land in Wisconsin had been taken except for one small reservation.

Although their land was gone, the tribes stayed in Wisconsin, opposing removal by dragging out negotiations over new land in the West. In 1849, the government abandoned removal in favor of locating reservations in small areas of lands the tribes had sold. The government stopped moving eastern tribes west of the Mississippi because of disagreements between Plains Indians and eastern Indians. The threat of inter-tribal warfare endangered settlers and discouraged expansion.

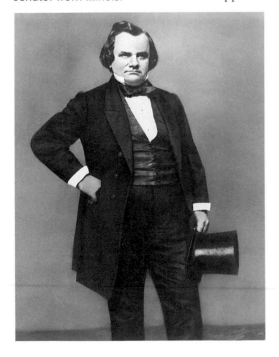

Stephen A. Douglas, senator from Illinois.

### Slavery and the Battle for Territorial Control

While Indians were being confined, European-Americans poured westward. Antislavery forces demanded that slavery be kept out of new territories, but southerners said slavery should not be barred from land belonging to the whole nation. If new states entered the Union as free states, the antislavery voice would be strengthened in Congress. But if new states came in as slave states, southern power might be regained. The surface issue was slavery, but the underlying, equally important, issue was political power.

Senator Stephen A. Douglas of Illinois pushed the Kansas-Nebraska Act through Congress in 1854. This bill established two new territories where the slavery question would be settled by "popular sovereignty." In other words, the territorial governments in Kansas and Nebraska would decide the question for themselves.

The North opposed the Kansas-Nebraska Act. Not only did the northern states want to keep slavery out of the territories, they also wanted to keep the West open for white labor. Opponents of the Kansas-Nebraska Act formed the Republican Party, which emerged as a strong force in the elections of 1856.

Even though the Supreme Court declared that Congress could not exclude slavery in the territories, northern Republicans refused to accept the decision and fought it in rallies, speeches, and editorials. They also fought it with violence. In Kansas, for example, two hundred people were killed by various vigilantes in 1856 alone. Small wonder that the new state became known as "Bloody Kansas."

Northern Senator Charles Sumner attacked by southern Congressman Preston Brooks on the Senate floor.

## Eve of War

Tensions in the 1850s were so great that a southern congressman, Representative Preston Brooks of South Carolina, beat a northern senator, Charles Sumner — a champion of the antislavery cause — with a cane during a disagreement on the Senate floor. Sumner was so injured by the beating that he could not return to Washington for three years. Meanwhile, Brooks was sent 180 replacement canes by supporters. Pieces of his broken cane were prized as souvenirs in the South.

The first slave's arrival in America in 1619 was indeed the war's seed, but the bitter harvest was not reaped until after Abraham Lincoln was elected president in 1860. He had run on an antislavery (but not an all-out abolitionist) Republican ticket. His candidacy so incensed the South that he was off the ballot in ten southern states. South Carolina adopted an Ordinance of Secession in December 1860, withdrawing from the nation shortly after Lincoln's election. Six other states — Mississippi, Florida, Alabama, Georgia, Louisiana, and Texas — withdrew before Lincoln's inauguration. In February 1861, representatives of the seven states met to establish a new nation, the Confederate States of America.

In his March 1861 inaugural, Lincoln did not mention war. But he noted that secession was illegal. He also said he would defend federal property in the South. When the Confederates fired on Fort Sumter in the harbor of Charleston, South Carolina, on April 12, he called on federal troops. The South saw this as a declaration of war, and Virginia, Arkansas, North Carolina, and Tennessee joined the Confederacy. The Civil War — a war that would take more American lives than any other, a war that would pit brother against brother and father against son, a war that would reduce the South to ruin — was about to begin.

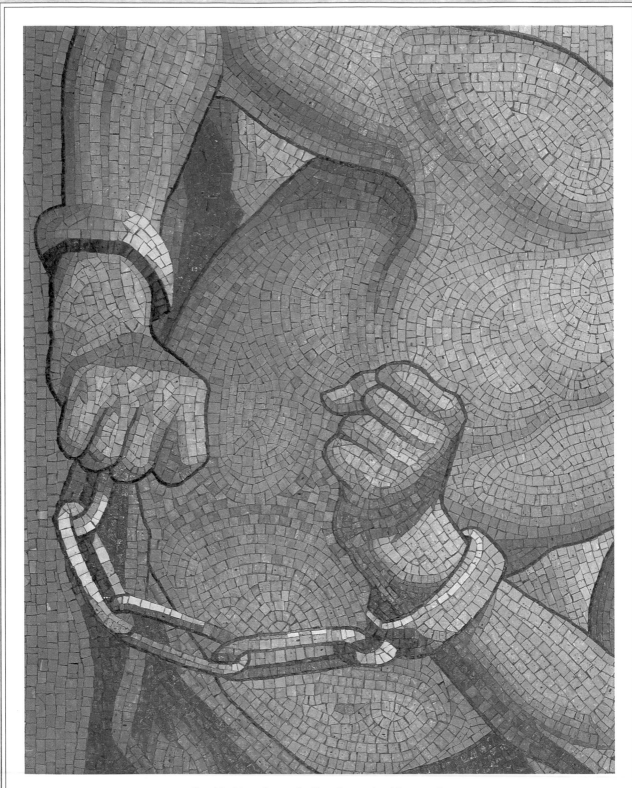

Shackled hands symbolize slavery in this mosaic.

# CHAPTER TWO

# Mapping the Road to Freedom

John Fairfield was the son of a wealthy Virginia slaveholder. But John hated slavery, could not stand living in a southern slave state, and eventually decided to live in a free state. Before moving North, he helped a slave friend escape to Canada. Other European-Americans in his community tried to track him down and arrest him. They did not find him, but slaves seeking freedom did, and Fairfield could not ignore their cries for help.

The youthful Virginian became a conductor on the Underground Railroad. Neither underground nor a railroad, this network of slaves, freed Blacks, and anti-slave whites secretly moved escapees from the South to free states in the North or to Canada. The Underground Railroad operated under that name for just twenty-one years — from 1840 to the start of the Civil War in 1861. But tales live on of danger and bravery associated with the lifeline that stretched from south to north.

Like most people associated with the Underground Railroad, Fairfield went to great lengths to accomplish his task, posing as a slaveowner or trader or a peddler of eggs and poultry to win the confidence of slaveholders. He was such a good actor that he was rarely suspected of helping escapees. He freed dozens of slaves in Louisiana, Alabama, Mississippi, Tennessee, and Kentucky. He once helped twenty-eight slaves elude capture by organizing them into a funeral procession!

John Fairfield even delivered escaped slaves to order. Blacks in the northern United States or in Canada gave him money for expenses and a description of friends or relatives. He found the people described and helped them flee their masters. Fairfield often traveled the entire route with escapees — hiding in woods by day and walking dark and seldom-traveled roads by night. He also delivered escapees to Levi Coffin, a Quaker living in Indiana and the unofficial president of the Underground Railroad. Coffin then arranged the rest of the journey.

Fairfield suffered from lack of food or sleep and from the effects of bad weather. During one escape, he was hit by gunfire. But he continued this dangerous work until his death in 1860, when he was killed during a slave revolt in Tennessee.

## Runaways on Their Own

Despite the efforts of slaveowners to discourage thoughts of freedom, many slaves refused to be held in bondage and took heroic measures to escape. Some forged

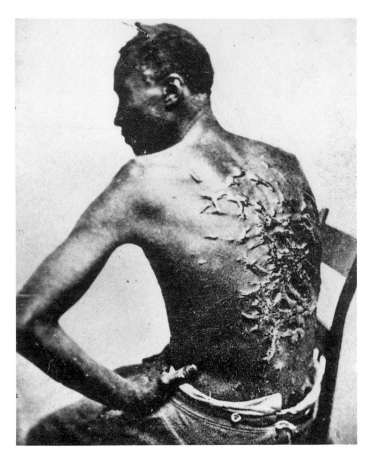

This slave's back bears the scars of a whipping.

passes or free papers. (Even though there were laws against literacy, a few slaves had learned to read and write.) In southern ports, slaves escaped by ship. They boarded with cargo or bundles of laundry, then hid below decks. Sometimes runaways organized themselves in groups called Maroons. These desperate people somehow survived for long periods in the forests, mountains, and swamps of the South, and while hidden from whites, some even formed themselves into Maroon settlements.

Other slaves simply walked off on their own, following the North Star. They took to the woods, walking by night and resting in swamps and other forbidding places by day. Slaves hid in piles of leaves, which helped them avoid detection and gave them some scant protection from the weather. Runaways ate berries, nuts, fruits, and an occasional stolen chicken. Slaves who lived near rivers stole away in canoes or on rafts. Despite brutal punishment for runaways who were caught, some slaves escaped again and again. One North Carolina woman's desperation was reflected in sixteen attempts to flee her master's plantation!

## The Price of Freedom

Runaways who were caught were subjected to punishment so severe that many slaves gave up after their first attempt. Whippings were standard, and professional slave breakers, cruel men who were hired to break a runaway's spirit, often punished runaways in front of a plantation's slave population, whipping or otherwise injuring the runaways to convey a message.

Many captured runaways were branded with molten iron. Others were sold away from the plantation, never to see their families again. Some plantations held captured runaways in dirty, cagelike jails. The most severe penalties included temporary starvation, amputation, or even death. Not surprisingly, such methods were rarely used, because they meant the loss of labor. While it has been argued that many more slaves would have run away if their punishment were not so brutal, many slaves preferred life on the run to life on the plantation, even with the risks of capture.

## Freedom Without Guarantees

Until 1850, African-Americans who escaped to the North could generally count on freedom for the rest of their lives. But with the passage of the federal Fugitive Slave Law, all that changed. This new law threw out sworn testimony of accused runaways. It assumed their guilt rather than their innocence. Blacks who had lived free for years could be captured by plantation owners or their agents and jailed. They had no way to defend themselves. The Fugitive Slave Law stripped escaped slaves of any freedom and dignity that they had fought to gain — but it also had the effect of helping keep alive the Underground Railroad.

Abolitionists used the new law as a powerful propaganda tool. Many northerners came to question slavery after hearing widespread stories of injustices done to free African-Americans. Abolitionists called the slave law the "man-stealing law" and the "bloodhound bill."

There was nothing, even in the early years of the United States, to insure freedom in the North. A federal law passed by Congress in 1793 allowed masters to reclaim escaped slaves in any state in the Union. Blacks were punished much more severely than whites for hiding escapees. Free Blacks found guilty of harboring slaves were

generally whipped, while whites faced only fines or imprisonment. A second offense for African-Americans might bring death. In Maryland, a free Black found guilty of providing freedom papers could be fined three hundred dollars (a huge sum at the time) or sold into seven years of labor if he or she had no cash to pay the fine.

Courage, confidence, and desperation were required to run away. Many runaways were skilled craftsworkers, mechanics, or servants. They often were literate, and some had even traveled widely. Despite many unfavorable attitudes and U.S. laws during the years leading up to the Civil War, all of these factors allowed them a chance at a successful life — if they could reach the North.

Two images illustrate the brutal treatment of slaves in the South.
*Top:* Tracking down fugitive slaves on their way north.
*Bottom:* A slave is punished by beating.

Colonel Benjamin Butler offered asylum to runaway slaves from Virginia.

## Wars and Runaways

Once the Civil War began, the number of runaways skyrocketed. Whenever Yankee troops drew near, African-Americans poured into their ranks. This phenomenon dates officially from May 23, 1861, when three Virginia runaways sought asylum at Fort Monroe. Colonel Benjamin Butler refused to return them to their master, and the news spread among slaves from one plantation to the next.

The military as a means of escape dated from the Revolutionary War, when slaves were lured to the British side with promises of freedom. Benjamin Harrison, a signer of the Declaration of Independence, lost thirty of his best slaves because of the British. Arthur Middleton of Charleston, South Carolina, also a signer of the Declaration of Independence, lost fifty slaves. Another South Carolinian, William Hazzard Wigg, lost ninety-six.

Slaveholders strengthened the slave-patrol system but could not stem the tide. In 1779, North Carolina gave those on patrol a tax cut and exemptions from roadwork, militia duty, and jury service. A 1778 Georgia law required one-third of the troops in every county to remain at home for permanent local control of slaves. Virginia masters were told to hide their slaves when British forces were near. Despite these efforts, tens of thousands of slaves reached British lines and one thousand bore arms for the British. When the Revolutionary War ended, the British evacuated around fifteen thousand Blacks from Charleston, New York City, and Savannah, Georgia, to England, Canada, and other British colonies.

## Refuge Among the Free

The larger the population of free Blacks, the more opportunities there were for escape. Free Blacks encouraged and aided the flight of slaves. Runaways took

### Slave revolts

Some slaves fought back by revolting rather than running away. They might slow up on their work, work inefficiently, pretend illness, or act as if they couldn't understand a task. They might be careless about property or damage farm instruments. They even started fires.

In extreme cases, enslaved African-Americans hurt themselves by cutting off fingers or hands, or even by committing suicide. There are also reports of slaves getting back at their masters by poisoning them or by putting ground glass in their food, such as in gravy.

Armed revolts happened, too. A revolt led by Nat Turner of Virginia in 1831 is probably the most famous. Many fellow slaves considered Turner a prophet, so when he decided to rebel, they followed. His revolt lasted for several weeks and spread terror among European-Americans in the South. Turner eventually was caught, tried, and hanged for playing a part in the deaths of fifty-one white people. Slaves thought to have been in Turner's ragtag army were killed as quickly as those who willingly followed their strong-willed leader. Turner's revolt is important because it put an end to the myth that slaves were content with their lowly position in life.

refuge with free friends and relatives so often that masters often looked there first when searching for escaped slaves.

Slaves escaped to gain freedom, but the individual reasons and circumstances surrounding their escape varied. Some fled to get back at a master for an increased workload; others escaped because of the sale of a loved one, or because of particularly severe punishment. The death of a master or the threat of being sold also might prompt a slave to risk escape.

Escape may have occurred merely because the slave needed rest. Hiding in the woods a few days was relatively easy and sometimes worth the pain that was sure to follow. Escape to freedom, on the other hand, required planning, assistance, and luck.

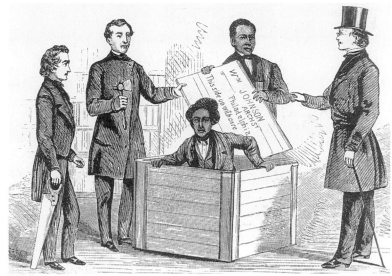

Henry Box Brown escapes to freedom in a wooden crate.

Most slaves were escorted to freedom by people who made up the loose Underground Railroad network of secret stations. In the early days, most fugitives were men, and they traveled on foot. As more women and children escaped, vehicles were provided. Conductors carried their human cargo in closed carriages, covered wagons, and farm wagons equipped with hidden compartments. Runaway slaves were sometimes put in boxes and shipped as freight by boat or rail. Henry Box Brown, for example, was shipped from Richmond to Philadelphia by the Adams Express Company. Conductors followed the Ohio and other rivers, mountain chains, and stars as they led their charges to freedom.

Stations on the Underground Railroad were ten to twenty miles apart. Runaways ate, rested, and awaited the next night's journey. During the day, escapees were hidden in attics, in barns, or in other out-of-the-way places. While runaways were hiding, conductors sent messages via the "grapevine telegraph," brief bits of information moving from one trusted neighbor to the next. These secret messages told stations down the line how many fugitives were coming. One message to the next station master in 1859 said, "By tomorrow evening's mail, you will receive two volumes of the *Irrepressible Conflict*, bound in black. After perusal, please forward and oblige." Obviously, two slaves rather than two books awaited nightfall to travel to the next station.

Plantation supplies were stolen and hoarded for planned escapes. Disguises were created from castoff clothing, and the ruses they devised were risky and often complex. If slaves had light complexions, they passed as whites — sometimes as their own masters. Slaves with darker skin posed as servants on the way to meet their owners. Runaways could be given white babies to hold at crucial moments to make them look like nurses. Women posed as men, and men posed as women.

The concept of aiding slaves who wanted to run away goes back to the early eighteenth century. In 1786, George Washington complained that one of his slaves had been helped to escape from Alexandria, Virginia, to Philadelphia

*Above:* Isaac T. Hopper moved to the North to help slaves escape the South. *Below:* Fugitive slaves arrive at Levi Coffin's home in Indiana.

by "a society of Quakers, formed for such purposes." In 1787, Isaac T. Hopper — though only a teenager — moved to Philadelphia for the sole purpose of helping slaves escape the South. Within a few years, the movement had grown, and slaves were being aided in a number of towns in Pennsylvania and New Jersey. This assistance slowly spread in various directions throughout the North.

The name *Underground Railroad* was probably coined when steam railroads became popular. One story giving the origins of the name tells how Tice Davis escaped across the Ohio River from his Kentucky master in 1831. Once Davis crossed the river, his master, in hot pursuit, could find no trace of him. It was as if Tice had "gone off on an underground road."

More than thirty-two hundred Americans were members of the Underground Railroad. Levi Coffin, the Quaker in the tiny town of Fountain City, Indiana, helped more than three thousand escapees. Calvin Fairbanks was another important member. He learned to hate slavery as a student at Oberlin College in northern Ohio. Traveling the South beginning in 1837, he transported slaves across the Ohio River from Kentucky. It was said that not one of his runaways was ever recaptured. Not all railroaders were men. A Vermont school teacher known only as Webster once helped three slaves escape when the runaways posed as her servants.

## Support for the Underground Railroad

Vigilance committees were founded by free Blacks to help runaways find homes and jobs and to protect them once they were settled. The secretary of the vigilance committee in Albany, New York, was a Black man named Steven Myers, a newspaper publisher and lobbyist. The corresponding secretary of the Philadelphia vigilance committee was William Sill, whose father had purchased freedom and whose mother had run away to the North.

Running the secret network cost money. Funds were needed for food, clothing, and sudden expenses such as the cost of a train ticket to get away from an owner in pursuit. Disguises were

## A mother writes her husband

This heartbreaking letter illustrates how slave families were thoughtlessly split up. The writer was a slave in Virginia, where the letter was written in 1852. Since slaves were forbidden to read or write, someone probably wrote the letter for the grieving woman. In turn, her husband probably took the letter to someone willing to read it to him.

Dear Husband I write you a letter to let you know my distress my master has sold albert to a trader on Monday court day and myself and other child is for sale also and I want you to let [me] hear from you very soon before next cort if you can I don't know when I don't want you to wait till Christmas I want you to tell dr hamelton and your master if either will buy me they can attend to it know and then I can go afterwards. I don't want a trader to get me they asked me if I had got any person to buy me and I told them no they took me to the court houste too they never put me up a man buy the name of brady bought albert and is gone I don't know where they say he lives in scottesville my things is in several places som is in staunton and if I should be sold I don't know what will become of them I don't expect to meet with the luck to get that way till I am quite heartsick — nothing more I m and ever will be your kind wife

Maria Perkins

also expensive, especially if a slave posed as a free and wealthy African-American. Vigilance committees in Pennsylvania and New York, Quaker societies, and similar groups raised money for the Underground Railroad. Philanthropists — wealthy people who give to worthy causes — gave money, as did conductors and other "officials." When she needed money for her underground work, the well-known Harriet Tubman would take a few months off and hire herself out as a domestic servant.

Young people also were involved, especially those who saw slavery as sinful. Students at Lane Theological Seminary in Ohio discussed slavery and became involved in their communities, organizing groups to help runaway slaves. They tutored African-Americans and participated in underground activities. When a conservative administration took charge of the seminary, many students left for the more progressive Oberlin College, also in Ohio, to continue fighting slavery.

Whether Blacks ran away on their own or used the support and assistance of the Underground Railroad, escape was often expensive and always dangerous. The risks that came with escape were great, and the immediate rewards were often meager. And yet the alternative "choice" — a monstrous system of bondage based on the idea that an entire group of human beings could be considered as nothing better than property, to be bought, sold, traded, and treated like animals — was no choice at all.

Calvin Fairbanks.

Abraham Lincoln (in wide-brimmed hat toward left) observes a slave auction in New Orleans.

# CHAPTER THREE

# Coming Together, Pulling Apart

As a nation that was still only a few decades old, the nineteenth-century U.S. was racing headlong out of its colonial past and into a period of incredible territorial growth. Grabbing land from its western frontier — and from the American Indians who inhabited it — the United States seemed to be devouring territory faster than it could absorb it. And yet, in the face of all this growth, other forces were afoot that would one day pull the young nation apart and thrust it into war against itself. From the 1840s up to the start of the Civil War in 1861, one issue had emerged to dominate the political landscape. That issue was slavery.

During his election campaign and throughout his term as president, Abraham Lincoln tried to make saving the Union, rather than abolishing slavery, the central issue of his presidency. But as the war progressed, and especially with Lincoln's issuing the Emancipation Proclamation in 1863, several things had become clear to the politicians, military leaders, and common folks of both North and South alike. The abolition of slavery had become a central issue of the war, and whoever won the war would also win the right to determine not only the political fate of the United States and Confederate States, but also whether slavery would live or die.

With the stakes — and emotions — so high for both sides, it should come as no surprise that many groups were formed to oppose or promote slavery in the years preceding the Civil War. As you will see in this chapter, the splitting apart of the Union was foreshadowed both by groups opposing one another and by splits *within* organizations as disagreements over slavery grew. Speakers and writers fanned the flames, and by 1861, the nation was set to explode.

## Abolitionism — Speaking Out Against Slavery

The first group of abolitionists, the Pennsylvania Society, was formed in 1775 in Philadelphia by organizers who felt that slavery was inconsistent with the ideals of the American Revolution. The group lost some of its momentum during the years of the Revolutionary War, but it was revived in April 1784, and New York organized a society of its own less than a year later. New Jersey was next, and by the end of 1790, societies had formed in Delaware, Maryland, Connecticut, and Rhode Island. The first national convention was held in Philadelphia in 1794,

# THE LIBERATOR.

**VOL. I.]** WILLIAM LLOYD GARRISON AND ISAAC KNAPP, PUBLISHERS. **[NO. 17.**

BOSTON, MASSACHUSETTS.] OUR COUNTRY IS THE WORLD—OUR COUNTRYMEN ARE MANKIND. [SATURDAY, APRIL 23, 1831.

### THE LIBERATOR

IS PUBLISHED WEEKLY
AT NO. 11, MERCHANTS' HALL.

**WM. LLOYD GARRISON, EDITOR.**

TERMS.

☞ Two Dollars per annum, payable in advance.
☞ Agents allowed every sixth copy.
☞ No subscription will be received for a shorter period than six months.
☞ All letters and communications must be POST PAID.

AGENTS.

CHARLES WHIPPLE, *Newburyport, Mass.*
JAMES E. ELLIS, *Providence, R. I.*
PHILIP A. BELL, *New-York City.*
JOSEPH CASSEY, *Philadelphia, Pa.*
HENRY OGDEN, *Newark, N. J.*
WILLIAM WATKINS, *Baltimore, Md.*

two committee men and a constable interfered, and would not permit him to take his seat! He was finally driven away, and the pew passed into other hands.

We purpose shortly to visit all our meeting-houses, and ascertain what places are provided for the accommodation of our colored people. A house dedicated to the worship of Almighty God, should be the last place for the exercise of despotic principles.— But here is the extract:

'With deep regret we have observed some articles in the columns of the "Liberator," of Boston, apparently from this city, in which its inhabitants are implicated; and which we believe the editor of that publication will deem very injudicious, as well as unkind, when knowing the truth in the case. So far from wishing to deprive the colored population of an opportunity to worship God, by the co-operation of the friends of religion with that part

be elevated and improved in this country; unanimous in opposing their instruction; unanimous in exciting the prejudices of the people against them; unanimous in apologising for the crime of slavery; unanimous in conceding the right of the planters to hold their slaves in a limited bondage; unanimous in denying the expediency of emancipation, unless the liberated slaves are sent to Liberia; unanimous in their hollow pretence for colonizing, namely, to evangelize Africa; unanimous in their *true motive* for the measure—a terror lest the blacks should rise to avenge their accumulated wrongs. It is a conspiracy to send the free people of color to Africa under a benevolent pretence, but really that the slaves may be held more securely in bondage. It is a conspiracy based upon fear, oppression and falsehood, which draws its aliment from the prejudices of the people, which is sustained by duplicity,

virtue. I doubt not this conviction will ultimately prevail in every community, where the obligations of religion and philanthropy are acknowledged; though the process may be slow; having to contend with much ignorance prejudice and error. This conviction, however, is but the first step towards a result so desirable as the total abolition of slavery. Every long established custom acquires a strong hold on the feelings of those who are habituated to its control; we know that its power in many cases is almost unconquerable; and this is especially the case, where a custom, however injurious in its tendencies, is a source of pecuniary emolument, or worldly aggrandizement to those interested in its continuance. It therefore becomes necessary for the attainment of this great and good object—the universal emancipation of our colored brethren—the complete overthrow of this abominable traffic in human flesh—to investigate the

*Top:* The masthead of William Lloyd Garrison's *Liberator* pictured an auction at which both slaves and horses were being sold.
*Bottom:* William Lloyd Garrison.

with ten state organizations. The leaders of these early abolitionists, men such as John Jay, were not hotheaded zealots, but men of property and standing. They were orderly, law-abiding, and well mannered.

As time passed, abolitionists demanded the immediate freedom of all slaves. Their sentiments were given a strong voice when New England journalist William Lloyd Garrison began printing *The Liberator* in Boston in 1831. There were four thousand subscribers to the antislavery newspaper in its first year, four hundred of whom were Blacks.

Garrison joined fifteen others to form the American Anti-Slavery Society. There were six African-Americans on the group's board and up to two hundred thousand members in the group as a whole. Garrison expressed his feelings with conviction — so much so that some people called him a fanatic and a radical. He burned a copy of the Constitution, calling it "an agreement with hell" because it permitted slavery. He called slavery a sin and slaveholders sinners.

Most southerners hated abolitionists, and the history of the nineteenth-century South is filled with incidents of anti-abolitionist violence against both abolitionist speakers and free African-Americans. A Georgian who subscribed to Garrison's paper was dragged from his home by a mob. He was tarred and feathered, set on fire, ducked into a river, tied to a post, and whipped. Somehow, he survived.

An anti-abolitionist mob set Garrison's house on fire and wrecked his printing presses. When Amos Dresser, a former seminary student from Ohio, went to Tennessee to sell Bibles, he was lashed by a mob one midnight in a public square. The mob believed he was spreading abolitionist doctrine and attacked Dresser when they could not prove their charges in court.

Southern whites who associated with African-Americans in any way suggesting equality were dealt with harshly. Several European-Americans in Georgia and South Carolina were murdered for the "crime" of mixing with Blacks in public. Most leading participants in the abolition movement as well as in the Underground Railroad could boast that they were officially wanted in the South.

Abolitionist voices grew, and as they became louder, more and more northerners believed the only time to end slavery was immediately. They had no patience for any plan that might delay freeing all slaves. Abolitionists were found in church groups, in women's rights groups, and in political groups. They were joined by people who were willing to be violent, to commit crimes, and to die for the freedom of slaves.

One of the most influential writers opposing slavery was Harriet Beecher Stowe, author of *Uncle Tom's Cabin*. She wrote the book to protest the Fugitive Slave Act of 1850, which stepped up efforts to return runaways to their masters. Men who had been free for years were snatched from their families and sent to the South, and bounties for returning runaways encouraged the wrongful capture of free Blacks.

*Below:* Harriet Beecher Stowe.
*Bottom:* A scene from *Uncle Tom's Cabin.*

*Uncle Tom's Cabin* was first serialized under a different title in an antislavery newsletter in 1851. It was published as a book in 1852. Many people turned against slavery because of Stowe's writing, and, in fact, *Uncle Tom's Cabin* became the antislavery movement's single most powerful piece of propaganda. It was an instant bestseller in the United States, and more than a million copies were sold in England in its first year of publication. Descriptions of the inhumane treatment of African-Americans struck a chord in the North that broadened the abolitionists' appeal.

### Quaker Leadership

Many early abolitionist groups were led by the Society of Friends, better known as Quakers, who organized antislavery groups in the South as well as in the North. Quakers believe that all life is sacred, and they emphasize inward spiritual experience rather than specific creeds. They have always been known as humanitarians, and they often work against war and racial barriers to human rights.

The Quakers, or Friends, came to North America from England in 1682 when William Penn founded the colony

## From *Uncle Tom's Cabin*

The following passage from Harriet Beecher Stowe's American classic offers one of many dramatic descriptions of slave life that turned increasing numbers of white Americans against slavery:

It was late in the evening when the weary occupants of the shanties came flocking home — men and women, in soiled and tattered garments, surly and uncomfortable, and in no mood to look pleasantly on new-comers. The small village was alive with no inviting sounds; hoarse, guttural voices contending at the handmills where their morsel of hard corn was yet to be ground into meal, to fit it for the cake that was to constitute their only supper. From the earliest dawn of the day, they had been in the fields, pressed to work under the driving lash of the overseer; for it was now in the very heat and hurry of the season, and no means was left untried to press every one up to the top of their capabilities.

"True," says the negligent lounger; "picking cotton isn't hard work." Isn't it? And it isn't much inconvenience, either, to have one drop of water fall on your head; yet the worst torture of the inquisition is produced by drop after drop, drop after drop, falling moment after moment, with monotonous succession, on the same spot; and work, in itself not hard, becomes so, by being pressed, hour after hour, with unvarying, unrelenting sameness, with not even the consciousness of free-will to take from its tediousness.

Tom looked in vain among the gang, as they poured along, for companionable faces. He saw only sullen, scowling, imbruted men, and feeble, discouraged women, or women that were not women — the strong pushing away the weak — the gross, unrestricted animal selfishness of human beings, of whom nothing good was expected and desired; and who, treated in every way like brutes, had sunk as nearly to their level as . . . possible. . . . To a late hour in the night the sound of the grinding was protracted; for the mills were few in number compared with the grinders, and the weary and feeble ones were driven back by the strong, and came on last in their turn. . . .

Tom waited till a late hour, to get a place at the mills; and then, moved by the utter weariness of two women, whom he saw trying to grind their corn there, he ground for them, put together the decaying brands of the fire, where many had baked cakes before them, and then went about getting his own supper. It was a new kind of work there — a deed of charity, small as it was; but it woke an answering touch in their hearts — an expression of womanly kindness came over their hard faces; they mixed his cake for him, and tended its baking; and Tom sat down by the light of the fire, and drew out his Bible — for he had need of comfort.

of Pennsylvania as a haven from religious persecution. Before they began speaking out against slavery, Quakers first freed their own slaves. They also paid American Indians for land, rather than simply taking it from them.

As early as the mid-1700s, Quaker John Woodman made a thoughtful observation about the attitudes of racism: "Placing on men the ignominious title, SLAVE, dressing them in uncomely garments, keeping them to servile labor, in which they are often dirty, tends generally to fix a notion in the Mind, that they are a sort of people below us in Nature, and leads us to consider them as such in all our Conclusions about them."

There was no other church group so unanimously abolitionist as the Quakers. But since Quakers also believed strongly in peaceful solutions rather than violence, they were excluded from leadership in the abolitionist movement as it became more militant.

## Other Religious Groups

There were other religious groups opposed to slavery. Mennonites began speaking out as early as 1680, and as the abolition movement grew between 1830 and 1850, Congregational-Presbyterians joined the ranks as well. Among the abolitionist leaders were many Methodists, some Baptists, and to a lesser degree, Episcopalians, Unitarians, and Catholics.

Not surprisingly, religious groups in the South were virtually unanimous in their defense of slavery. Even in the North, many people who belonged to churches supported slavery. Abolitionist activity was not considered the business of most churches.

Some religious groups, such as the Baptists, Methodists, and Presbyterians, had difficulty in dealing with antislavery issues at national gatherings because church members were from both the North and the South. Some churches actually split over the issue. Methodists in 1844 told Bishop James O. Andrew of Georgia that he could not perform his duties so long as he was a slaveholder. This

A temporary home for a group of Russian Mennonites.

proved unacceptable to southern church members, so the church separated into southern and northern Methodists. A similar split took place in the Baptist church when northern members spoke against missionaries who owned slaves.

Southern churches offered spiritual leadership within the existing social order, so they didn't want to overthrow the social system, which was based on slavery. Preaching slavery to a southern congregation was a safe thing to do, since by 1800 African-American and European-American Baptists and Methodists worshipped separately, and white southern ministers had little fear of offending their congregants. In the North, ministers could preach against

## John Brown

Abolition leader John Brown may have been a zealot, but he had a sense of humor. When President Buchanan offered a $250 reward for his head, Brown posted a $250 reward on the head of Buchanan!

Brown was widely known even before he attacked and briefly held the federal arsenal at Harper's Ferry, Virginia, in 1859. The New England resident and father of twenty-two children grew tired of waiting for the government to act and led a ragtag bunch of sons, Blacks, misfits, extremists, and adventurers to Kansas. There, the gang not only killed several pro-slavery residents, but hacked them to bits.

Brown and friends and family stormed the Virginia arsenal on Oct. 16, 1859. The abolitionist believed Blacks would head for the arsenal, arm themselves, and begin the titanic struggle for freedom. It didn't happen. Instead, Robert E. Lee and J. E. B. Stuart, both U.S. Army officers at the time, arrived with troops who assaulted the building. Because the South feared slave revolts as they feared little else, Virginia tried, convicted, and hanged Brown before year's end. (In the picture, left, the bearded John Brown is led to his execution.) His death and martyrdom further split North and South, leading to secession and war two years later.

slavery without threatening the existing order, since the North's social and economic system was not based on slavery.

Jews, like people of most other religions and cultures, were divided over slavery and secession. There were 150,000 Jews in the United States by 1861, mostly in the North and West but also in the South. Although they would experience prejudice and discrimination during the Civil War, prewar southern Jews enjoyed more opportunities and acceptance than elsewhere in the country. Jews who moved south quickly discovered that skin color, not origin or religious preference, was what mattered most. Jews who owned slaves defended the practice, and Jews who didn't often failed to criticize the practice. Some Jews were slave traders and thus had their own reasons for supporting slavery.

Other Jews spoke out against slavery. One northern Jewish leader, Rabbi David Einhorn of Baltimore, was so strident that a secessionist mob destroyed his congregation's newspaper and forced him out of town. Fellow Jews worried that Einhorn's strong stand would endanger their otherwise peaceful lives in Maryland. In 1861, his own congregation asked him to leave town! The Einhorn family moved to Philadelphia and did not return to Baltimore after the war ended.

There were others. St. Louis politician Isidor Busch was one of the Midwest's most dynamic abolitionists, a particularly courageous position to take in a pro-slave state like Missouri. And August Bondi was a Jew who joined John Brown in the famed abolitionist's war against those who would enslave their fellow humans.

Most rabbis did not believe that Jews should oppose slavery. Like many other Jews, they had learned to be afraid of group passions when they found themselves at the mercy of anti-Semitic Europeans. It was not common for them to speak out at the time, and slavery was not seen as a religious issue.

## Women and Abolition

Included in the growing number of white people who became abolitionists was a large group that suffered many injustices of slavery in their own lives. Most middle-class women had always stayed at home while men took care of politics and decision-making, but by the mid-1800s, women began to speak in favor of both abolition and women's rights. People such as Angelina Grimké, Margaret Fuller, and Sojourner Truth called attention to the fact that white men treated women as slaves. Women weren't allowed to own property, weren't admitted to college, were rarely hired for good jobs, and couldn't vote. In fact, many women were treated as property by the men in their lives, first by their fathers and later by their husbands.

Women's rights differed from state to state, just as slave laws differed. For example, in some states a working woman had to give any money she earned to her husband. Husbands could legally beat their wives in some states, just as slaveholders were permitted to beat slaves. Divorce was rare, but if a couple did divorce, the wife could not keep the children.

All European-American adult males had been given the right to vote in 1824. That meant the United States was becoming somewhat more democratic. Yet the vote was withheld from women, slaves, and Amer-

### Angelina Grimké

It must have startled the all-male Massachusetts legislature to see a woman before them during an 1838 session — and a southern woman, at that. But there she was — Angelina Grimké, at one time a member of an aristocratic, slave-owning family, now a Quaker and an abolitionist. Grimké begged legislators to end slavery and to allow women to speak out politically. Until this time, few men had ever heard a woman speak in public.

Angelina and her sister Sarah presented the legislature with a petition signed by twenty thousand women who demanded an end to slavery. The petition was a landmark because, although women had been active in religious and social activities and had worked to achieve reforms in education, prisons, and hospitals, they seldom took a political stand.

Grimké's powers of persuasion didn't stop there. She composed a thirty-six-page pamphlet entitled "An Appeal to Christian Women of the South." It pointed out that slavery was anti-Christian and therefore should be overthrown. The Grimké sisters were threatened with death if they ever returned to the South Carolina of their childhoods.

Grimké is important because she and her sister, through speaking and writing, were able to connect the issues of women's rights and abolition. Many later women's rights advocates such as Elizabeth Cady Stanton and Susan Anthony were inspired by the two courageous sisters.

*Left:* Sojourner Truth.
*Right:* Margaret Fuller.

ican Indians. Only a few states allowed free African-Americans to vote. Though women of this era might have been working for their own suffrage, many female activists, especially in the North, were more concerned about slavery.

## The Irish and Slavery

Nearly half of the 4 million immigrants who came to America from 1830 to 1850 were Irish men, women, and children. They fled Ireland after a blight ruined the potato crop, causing starvation and 2 million deaths. Most Irish families who moved to the United States were poor Roman Catholic farmers. They had suffered discrimination by British Protestants, who saw Irish Catholics as inferior. Not surprisingly, the same kind of discrimination greeted these new Americans on this side of the Atlantic, particularly when they entered the labor force. Many Irish-Americans were so eager to work that they accepted low pay, thereby giving employers an excuse to lower everyone's wages. Workers born in the United States were angry about getting less money — and about the fact that immigrants were getting so many jobs.

The average Irish immigrant quickly became loyal to the new country. These immigrants were welcomed by relatives and friends and were eager to enter into the mainstream of life in the U.S. immediately upon their arrival. Most Irish immigrants adapted to the views of the region they now called home. Those who

### Experiment in Liberia

Repatriation — returning people to their native lands — was tried with American slaves. The story begins with the American Colonization Society, an organization formed in 1817 to free and transport slaves to the west coast of Africa. This ill-fated effort, which was fiercely debated by Black abolitionists, generally supported by slaveholders, and tried earlier by the British after the American Revolution, was based on a misunderstanding. The misunderstanding was simple: African-Americans believed they had purchased land from African chiefs, whereas the chiefs assumed they had merely lent them the land. Violence teamed with disease and lack of food to discourage the former Americans as they settled into their new homeland. Yet the newcomers introduced free elections and other democratic ideas to this land, which they named Liberia (literally, Free Country). Joseph Jenkins Roberts, born free in the U.S., was the country's first Black governor.

Not all American Blacks favored the establishment of Liberia, which became a republic in 1847. They feared the colony would become a dumping ground for U.S. whites to send Black criminals. White southerners wondered if Liberia wasn't another northern trick to end slavery. By 1865, however, there were more than 5 million African-Americans in the United States and only a few thousand returnees to Africa.

Liberians today are overwhelmingly African, though people of American descent — called Americo-Liberians — have run the country and, at times, discriminated against their African fellow citizens. Not even a brief "Back to Africa" movement by progressive Blacks early in this century raised Liberia's living standard, which remains poor. Nor did it bring stability to Liberia's government, which can change rapidly and violently.

lived in the North were against slavery. Though they were Democrats and were therefore linked politically to the Democrats of the South, they answered Republican President Abraham Lincoln's appeal to fight for the Union. And although most Irish who lived in the South didn't necessarily believe in slavery, like other southerners they felt that states should be able to rule without outside interference.

## Nativists and Know-Nothings

Most northerners were opposed to slavery, and, like the Irish, favored preserving the Union against the secession of southern states. And yet many whites in the North — particularly poor whites — did not exactly welcome Blacks with open arms. Many northerners thought an influx of former slaves would jeopardize their jobs, and there were laws and practices that reflected this hostility toward

### Frederick Douglass

Born a slave, Frederick Douglass rose to become a famous public speaker and the publisher of an antislavery newspaper, *The North Star*. Douglass escaped from his Maryland master in 1838 by fleeing to Bedford, Massachusetts. Born Frederick Augustus Washington Bailey, he dropped his two middle names and changed his last name to avoid detection. He worked as a ship caulker, a rubbish collector, and a digger of cellars.

After three years of freedom, Douglass gave a rousing speech at a meeting of the Massachusetts Antislavery Society, and his career as a speaker was launched. The society was so impressed that they hired him to speak on a regular basis.

In 1845, he published his autobiography, *Narrative of the Life of Frederick Douglass*. As his fame grew, he became afraid that he might be captured as a runaway slave. He departed for England, where he lectured and studied. Supporters there helped him raise money to buy his freedom, should the need arise. Returning home in 1847, he continued his fight against the enslavement of other men and women.

A consultant to President Lincoln during the war, Douglass advocated arming slaves in areas newly captured by Union forces. He outlived slavery in the U.S. by thirty years and is important because he spread the message concerning the horrors of slavery. He matters, too, because he proved, back when proof was needed, that African-Americans could operate successfully in a society that was predominantly European-American.

African-Americans. In New York, for example, all forms of transportation were segregated, as were public facilities. To a large extent, housing was segregated as well. Some American-born whites also became hostile toward immigrants. They feared the newcomers would ruin the "American way of life" because of their different languages and traditions and, in some cases, religions.

During the first half of the nineteenth century, nativists (people born in the United States) worked hard in secret societies to keep immigrants and Catholics out of politics and power. One nativist secret society, the Supreme Order of the Star-Spangled Banner, organized a new U.S. political party that had a strange pledge. It promised to answer all questions about party activities with the phrase "I don't know." This group became known as the Know-Nothings.

Nativists managed to elect several governors and senators, but by the 1856 presidential election, the Know-Nothings, like so many other groups, were split on the slavery issue. Northern Know-Nothings supported the newly formed antislavery Republican Party, while the southern Know-Nothings voted for compromise candidate Millard Fillmore.

Abraham Lincoln summed up his understanding of the Know-Nothing platform in 1855 as follows: "As a nation we began by declaring that 'All men are created equal.' We now practically read it, 'All men are created equal except Negroes.' When the Know-Nothings get control it will read, 'All men are created equal except Negroes and foreigners and Catholics.'"

## Vigilance Committees

African-Americans in dozens of northern communities formed vigilance committees to stop or slow down slave catchers and to help runaways. One vigilante was David Ruggles, who in 1827 came to New York from his Connecticut home at the age of just seventeen. Described as a dark and athletic man with "an intelligent and benevolent" appearance, Ruggles lived by selling everything from butter to books. But his real purpose in life was the Black struggle. He rescued slaves, found them hiding places, and got them jobs. He was a key member of New York's vigilance committee in 1835, when he was only twenty-five years old. Pro-slavery forces burned down his bookstore and reading room, probably because he attempted to teach slaves to read. Yet he continued the fight against slavery, despite at least one attempt to kidnap him. Ruggles's courageous acts included boarding ships to search for slaves being illegally smuggled into the country.

Ruggles kept the stream of African-Americans flowing into New York when he took in Frederick Augustus Washington Bailey. In time, he also brought in a clergyman to secretly perform a marriage ceremony for Bailey and his new wife. Ruggles then sent the couple to Massachusetts, where Bailey took on a new name, Frederick Douglass. Douglass became one of the strongest anti-slavery advocates ever. In time, Douglass, Ruggles, and other vigilantes joined and provided leadership to the abolitionist movement.

Blacks in the North faced great danger, since it was considered civil disobedience for anyone to offer food, clothing, hiding places, or transportation to runaways. Yet they were willing to lie to authorities, stare blankly into the faces of search parties, rescue fugitives from slave catchers, and help in any way possible in the ongoing struggle.

The vigilance committees and other African-Americans who worked for freedom did so with a strong sense of religious dedication. This resolution, written in 1835, vividly portrays their feelings: "Our duty to God, and to the principles of human rights, so far exceeds our allegiance to those laws that return the slave again to his master. . . that we recommend our people peaceably bear the punishment those [laws] inflict, rather than aid in returning their brethren again to slavery."

## A Nation Ready for War

With such tensions over so many issues — slavery, the struggle for political power between North and South, the pressures of immigration, competition for jobs, continued westward expansion, and the debate over whether new territories should be slave or free — it is not surprising that civil war broke out. If the differences dividing the nation had not been deep and strong, the commitment to fight over them might not have been so great. For the Civil War became the nation's bloodiest series of battles. Of two armies with the combined manpower of slightly more than 3 million, a staggering total of 618,000 would be killed.

Had the first seventy-five thousand Union troops called by President Lincoln read the following description written by an anonymous private, they might have abandoned the cause: "The day was terribly hot, and the troops suffered from lack of water, which was hard to get, and was mostly obtained from stagnant ponds, and that mixed with blood of the dead or dying soldiers and horses. All we had to eat was blackberries picked upon the battlefield. . . . Now that the conflict was over . . . perhaps a thousand soldiers lay cold in death — the blue and the gray side by side — while hundreds lay wounded, unable to aid themselves, pleading for help and almost famished from lack of water. Many with an arm or leg shattered, and weak from loss of blood and suffering intense agony, begged to be put out of their misery. . . ."

Recruited to serve for just three months, the troops quickly saw that the war — and bloody battle scenes like the one described above — would last for years. Americans were about to set upon one another like never before or since.

Dead soldiers on the battlefield at Gettysburg.

A Black Union infantry corporal.

# CHAPTER FOUR

# The War Years — 1861-1865

Johnny Clem ran away from Newark, Ohio, at the age of nine to join the Union Army. A drummer boy with the 22nd Michigan, he saw major battles at Shiloh, Perryville, Murfreesboro, and Atlanta. But he became famous at the Battle of Chickamauga in Tennessee.

A Confederate colonel charged Johnny on horseback, shouting at him to surrender. Rather than give up, Clem shot the enemy soldier. Benjamin Taylor reported the event in his Civil War memoirs, written in 1875: "A few swift moments ticked off by musket shots, and the tiny gunner was swept up at a swoop and borne away a prisoner. Soldiers, bigger but not better, were taken with him, only to be washed back again by a surge of Federal troopers, and the prisoner of thirty minutes was again John Clem 'of ours,' and General Rosecrans made him a Sergeant, and the stripes of rank covered him all over like a mouse in a harness, and the daughter of Mr. Secretary Chase presented him a silver medal appropriately inscribed, which he worthily wears, a royal order of honor, upon his left breast, and all men conspire to spoil him, but, since few ladies can get at him here, perhaps he may be saved."

Clem was appointed a second lieutenant in the postwar Army, where he served until 1915. He was a major general when he retired at sixty-five and was the last man active in the armed forces who had fought in the Civil War.

## Citizen Soldiers

Boys did serve in the Civil War, but they were the exception rather than the rule. The soldiers who fought the war were mostly older teens or young adults. They came from all walks of life — they were clerks, shopkeepers, farmers, blacksmiths, tailors, and schoolboys. In Philadelphia, recruiters took high school boys by the class. They were considered graduates once they went off to fight.

If it hurts to think of young boys on the battlefield, some pity should be reserved for America's newest citizens. Unknown numbers of immigrants, most of whom could neither read nor write English, were inducted into the Union Army. These unfortunate people had never touched a weapon before being briefly trained as infantry and ordered to charge enemy lines. Rifles and cannon firing grapeshot cut down young Italians, Germans, Poles, and Slavs by the hundreds.

A youthful "powder monkey" set explosives on board this ship during the Civil War.

Life on either side of the front was harsh, but most Confederate soldiers at least spoke the same language!

Recruitment was an important way of raising a fighting force because, in 1861, the U.S. Army had only sixteen thousand men. They were stationed in seventy-nine isolated posts across two thousand miles of frontier, mostly west of the Mississippi River. The Navy had forty-two vessels, but only twelve ships were immediately available. No plans had been made for mobilizing a national force, and there was no one to guide military activities. When war began on April 12, 1861, more than one-third of all officers resigned to join the Confederacy.

Americans at first answered the call to arms willingly. Patriotic enthusiasm ran high, and volunteers were plentiful. But as the war dragged on, recruitment become difficult. Many different techniques, ranging from a draft to the promise of cash, were used to attract manpower. Some whites responded bitterly to the call to arms. They thought it unfair to risk their lives to free southern Blacks. In July 1863, New York City whites in poor neighborhoods rioted. Many African-Americans were killed, and an orphans' home for Black children was burned to the ground.

## African-American Volunteers

Some 180,000 Blacks volunteered throughout the war. This represented between 9 and 10 percent of the total Union enlistments. They took part in 499 military engagements, 39 of which were major battles. Their mortality rate was high — 37,000 Black soldiers died. This represented 20 percent of all Black enlistees. Another 200,000 African-American men worked as teamsters, laborers, dock workers, and guides. African-American women served as laborers, nurses, spies, and guides. Sergeant William H. Carney of the 54th Massachusetts Volunteer Infantry was one of twenty-three Blacks to win Congressional Medals of Honor.

African-Americans volunteered from the start. On April 15, 1861, Lincoln issued a call for seventy-five thousand men after learning that Fort Sumter had been seized. The next day, a group of Boston Blacks, meeting in the Twelfth Baptist Church, pledged to President Lincoln their lives and fortunes. In Providence, a Black company offered to march with the First Rhode Island Regiment. In New York, three regiments of Black men were offered to the governor, along with the promise that African-Americans would finance arms and equipment and pay the soldiers. Philadelphia Blacks formed two regiments, and Blacks in Cleveland offered money, prayers, and manpower to win the war.

Captain O. C. Wood and thirty-five members of the Detroit Military Guard tried to enlist as soon as the smoke cleared over Fort Sumter. Dr. G. P. Miller of

Battle Creek, Michigan, asked the War Department permission to raise 5,000-10,000 freemen. Among the last of the letters written by African-American volunteers was one to President Lincoln from clergyman J. Stella Martin, who had returned to Boston from a lecture tour in England. He wrote, "If I can be of any means of service here, should your excellency ever think it best to employ my people, I am ready to work or preach or fight to put down this rebellion."

In the beginning, African-Americans were not accepted for military service. Jacob Dodson, a Black U.S. Senate attendant who had seen service with John C. Frémont in crossing the Rockies, offered three hundred Blacks to defend the nation's capital. He was told the War Department did not want colored soldiers. This was somewhat surprising, since Blacks had served during the Revolutionary War. They fought in the North and made weapons, drove wagons, built forts, repaired roads, and destroyed enemy bridges in the South.

Only after the Battle of Antietam in September 1862, when Lincoln announced his intention to issue the Emancipation Proclamation, did the North allowed Blacks to enlist. Recruitment had become difficult, and Blacks helped fill quotas. Northern governors saw African-American enlistments as a solution to recruiting woes, as did some white men who had been drafted. These European-American draftees sought substitutes because it was legal to pay others to serve in their place.

As rebel states came under the Union flag, freshly freed African-Americans joined the cause. In fact, northern states and private agents competed for recruits. After March 25, 1863, they also

Black Union troops photographed in 1865, toward the end of the Civil War.

Posing with musket, bayonet, and cartridge box, this American Indian was a private for the Union Infantry during the Civil War.

Black Union troops storm the Confederate barricades at Fort Wagner.

had to compete with the federal government. The government sent Adjutant General Lorenzo Thomas of the Union Army to the Mississippi Valley to organize Black troops. In less than three months, he raised twenty regiments, a force of almost twenty-five thousand men.

## Serving with Distinction

African-Americans served the country well, distinguishing themselves in battles such as Port Hudson on the lower Mississippi. Hudson was the last remaining Confederate fort on the lower part of the big river. Confederates had twenty siege guns and thirty pieces of artillery, posing a real threat to Union warships. Knocking out the fort would be a great help to troops under General Ulysses S. Grant at nearby Vicksburg, Mississippi. Five Black Louisiana regiments assaulted Fort Hudson but were met by a rain of bullets. Losses were severe — in one regiment, six successive flag bearers fell. The assaults failed, but no one questioned African-American bravery. "No body of troops — Western, Eastern, or rebel — have fought better in the war," reported *The New York Times*.

Milliken's Bend, Louisiana, a little town where Union troops were stationed twenty miles from Vicksburg, also is famous in African-American military history. It was manned by 1,410 Union soldiers, of whom only 160 were white. The rest were former Louisiana and Mississippi slaves who had joined the Army only sixteen days earlier. Confederate forces struck suddenly, rushing up and over the fort's entrenchments. Fierce, hand-to-hand bayonet fighting followed, the longest of the Civil War. Union forces won after one of their warships, the *Choctaw*, arrived on the scene.

Equally courageous Confederates retreated, leaving behind 130 dead — all the rebel ambulances were filled. Union casualties were heavy as well, totaling 652 killed, wounded, or missing. But the garrison's defenders had not backed down. "It is impossible for men to show greater gallantry than the Negro troops in this fight," General Elias S. Dennis told the assistant secretary of war. In his memoirs, Ulysses S. Grant wrote, "These men were very raw, but they behaved well."

Another battle in which Blacks distinguished themselves was at Fort Wagner, South Carolina, on July 18, 1863. A strong Confederate fortress on Morris Island controlled sea approaches to Charleston. In an attempt to take the fort, an assault was mounted with the Massachusetts 54th, the first Black regiment recruited in the North, leading the way. They were commanded by a white colonel, a twenty-five-year-old "Boston blue blood" and abolitionist named

Robert Gold Shaw. Shaw was convinced that African-American troops could fight as well as anyone, and he lost his life in the shadow of the fortress trying to prove it.

The Union attackers passed through a narrow area between sand hills and the sea, where a Confederate ambush lay in wait. The assault was doomed. Union forces fell back with heavy casualties, 1,515 men killed or wounded, compared to 174 dead or wounded Confederate troops. Yet the 54th's bravery under fire was praised throughout the North, and a sergeant, William Carney, became the first Black man to win the Medal of Honor. The battle remains in modern memory, and a Hollywood movie, *Glory*, recounts the deeds of the fighting 54th.

An African-American child named Johnny Aaron sits astride the horse of General John Rawling in Virginia, 1864.

Though they served with distinction, African-Americans were often discriminated against in northern units. Their enlistment period was longer, they had little chance of promotion, they were given old weapons, and their pay was lower than that of whites. Wounded Black soldiers were carried from the battlefield almost as an afterthought. If they arrived alive at a hospital, they received poor, slow care. And if a Black was captured by the Confederates, he was either immediately executed or treated as a runaway slave rather than as a war prisoner.

Union Army Blacks thus often fought with a greater sense of purpose and had better morale than white Union troops. There were deserters (nearly fifteen thousand have been recorded), but most served with honor. Secretary of War Edwin N. Stanton noted in a letter to President Lincoln in 1864 that "At Milliken's Bend, Port Hudson, Morris Island and other battlefields, they have proved themselves among the bravest of the brave, performing deeds of daring and shedding their blood with a heroism unsurpassed by soldiers of any other race."

While the Army barred Blacks from enlisting before the Emancipation Proclamation, the Navy was open to free Blacks. In September 1861, the Navy signed former slaves because of the constant shortage of men, and their manpower was used in immensely effective blockades of southern ports. By the end of the war, African-Americans made up one-quarter of the men in the Union fleet. The Navy treated its twenty-nine thousand Blacks well, quartering and feeding them with whites and offering some opportunities for promotion.

The best known of four African-American sailors awarded the Medal of Honor was Joachim Pease, loader on the number one gun of the *Kearsarge*. He was among fifteen Black sailors aboard when they met the *Alabama*, the most famous of the Confederate raiders, in a historic sea battle off the coast of France. The *Alabama* had captured sixty-nine northern ships in two years of operating all over

The *Kearsarge* and *Alabama* in a battle off the coast of France, 1864.

the Atlantic. Confronted west of the port of Cherbourg, the more heavily armed *Kearsarge* sunk the faster southern vessel. Pease was cited for his courage.

## Southern Black Enlistment

Only toward the end of the war was there serious talk of enlisting Blacks in the South. Once he knew that his young republic was losing, President Jefferson Davis decided to enlist African-Americans. Talking to officers in the Army of the Tennessee, he said, "...the experience of this war has been so far that half-trained Negroes have fought as bravely as many other half-trained Yankees." At that point of the Civil War, he would have offered freedom to slaves who enlisted.

The war ended before such a plan could be put in effect. That is just as well, since Davis's proposal had many opponents. One southerner said, "I think that the proposition to make soldiers of our slaves is the most pernicious idea that has been suggested since the war began.... You cannot make soldiers of slaves or slaves of soldiers. . . . The day you make soldiers of them is the beginning of the end of the revolution. If slaves make good soldiers, our whole theory of slavery is wrong."

Despite such sentiments and whatever "theories" of slavery

A recruiting poster encourages Blacks to enlist in the Union Army.

that lay behind them, however, African-Americans living in the South supported the war effort throughout the conflict, willingly or not. They built forts, cooked, tended animals, carried supplies, and performed hundreds of jobs that freed European-American southerners to fight.

They were often encouraged in their thoughts of freedom by free Blacks fighting in the Union Army. Even though most Blacks in the South did not rise up against their masters during the Civil War, many harbored the hope that war would free them. The presence of free northern Blacks buoyed that hope. Northern Black soldiers provided encouragement by singing,

> Don't you see the lightning?
> Don't you hear the thunder?
> It isn't the lightning,
> It isn't the thunder,
> It's the buttons on
> The Negro uniforms.

Another song popular with African-American soldiers was sung to the tune of "The Battle Hymn of the Republic":

> We are done with hoeing cotton,
> We are done with hoeing corn,
> We are colored Yankee soldiers,
> As sure as you are born.
> When Massa hears us shouting,
> He will think 'tis Gabriel's horn,
> As we go marching on.

Still, only about 10 percent of the slave population deserted their masters, more at the end of the war than the beginning. They supported the North indirectly with work slowdowns, a subtle form of resistance, but most waited to be delivered by Union troops. One dramatic escape was made by Robert Smalls and a band of fellow African-Americans in 1862. Noting that the officers of the steam-powered ship *The Planter* were ashore, the Blacks sailed the vessel past Confederate

## Rations

A letter written by Mary Phinney, a Union Army nurse, tells what food in a military camp was like: "I thought it best not to trouble you with an account of how we have been living lately — everything cut off, nothing but coffee (so poor and with hardly ever milk) and dry bread for breakfast; for dinner bread and meat (and such meat!). Always the tail or neck or some other nasty part, and at night coffee and bread again. . . .

"One day it was past all bearing. I was positively so hungry I could have eaten cat's meat. I sat over the fire after supper, tired and hungry and wondering if the good I did was balanced by my suffering. . . ."

## Army pets

Benjamin Taylor's memoirs tell about the unusual pets the soldiers kept in camp: "They have the strangest pets in the army, that nobody would dream of 'taking to' at home, and yet they are the little touches of the gentler nature that gives you some such cordial feeling when you see them, as there is in the clasp of a friendly hand. . . . One of the boys has carried a red squirrel 'through the thick and thin' over a thousand miles. 'Bun' eats hard-tack like a veteran, and has the freedom of the tent.

"Another's affections overflow upon a slow-winking, unspeculative little owl, captured in Arkansas, and bearing a name with a classical smack to it — Minerva. A third gives his heart to a young Cumberland mountain bear. But chief among camp pets are dogs. Riding on the saddle-bow, tucked into a baggage-wagon, mounted on a knapsack, growling under a gun, are dogs brought to a premature end as to ears and tails, and yellow at that. . . ."

batteries and safely into Union hands. "I thought," said Smalls, a future Congressman from South Carolina, "that *The Planter* might be of some use to Uncle Abe."

## Irish in the War

More than 144,000 Irish-born Americans served in the Union Army. Many were driven to enlist because, at the time, there was intense anti-Irish and anti-Catholic feeling in northern cities. Not only were Irishmen fighting oppression (something they had just fled Europe to escape), but many hoped to gain military experience in America that would help them win freedom back home. Most, but not all, were poor. Included in the Irish Brigade were writers, surgeons, teachers, students, lawyers, and journalists.

A smaller but still sizeable number of Irishmen fought for the South. Specifically, one southerner in nine was foreign born, and a goodly percentage of the population was of Irish descent. Like German Catholics who moved south, many Irish became Protestant and were quickly absorbed in the general European-American population. Pat Cleburne and Richard Dowling were two of hundreds of Irish-born Confederates. Cleburne was a highly rated division commander whose career declined after he advocated training slaves to fight for the Confederacy. Dowling, a saloon keeper, raised and led a company of Irish Catholic immigrants from Houston.

## Women at War

Women were not allowed to enlist in the military, but they became involved in other ways. Union women ran businesses and farms at home, wrote letters to elevate the spirits of their loved ones, raised money for equipment and medical supplies, and served as nurses and teachers. Some

Women caring for the wounded and sick.

northern women went south to teach ex-slaves to read in captured regions. One of the best known was Charlotte Forten, who was educated in Massachusetts and knew many reformers of the day, including John Greenleaf Whittier, Charles Sumner, and William Lloyd Garrison. She worked on St. Helena Island in the Sea Islands region of South Carolina.

In his memoirs, Civil War veteran Benjamin Taylor provides an appreciative description of women's efforts on the front: "You have been thinking, my sisters, where is *our* work in all these scenes? That snowy roll of linen; that little pillow beneath the sufferer's head; that soft fold across the gashed breast; that cooling drink the rude, kind, stalwart nurse is putting to yonder boy's white lips; that delicacy this poor fellow is just partaking of; that dressing-gown whose broidered hem those long, thin fingers are toying with; the slippers, a world too wide for the thin, faltering feet; the dish of fruit a left hand is slowly working at, his right laid upon our Federal altar at Chickamauga, never to be lifted more. *Your* tree, my sister, bore that fruit; *your* fingers wrought, your heart conceived."

Confederate women did many of the same tasks as their Union counterparts. They managed farms, raised money, sewed, clerked, nursed — and worked as spies. They waited for news of fathers, sons, husbands, and lovers. They buried the dead and cared for the wounded. They also provided some of the most poignant chronicles of the war, as demonstrated in the passage on page 52 taken from Mary A.H. Gay's memoirs, *Life in Dixie During the War*.

Blacks voting during Reconstruction.

## Blacks on the Home Front

Fully understanding the profound consequences of a Union victory on the lives of all African-Americans, free and slave, northern free Blacks worked passionately and tirelessly to influence public opinion in favor of African-American interests. Black spokesmen prodded mayors, governors, and congressmen to back the war. They kept up efforts to influence President Lincoln, first by encouraging him to permit Black enlistment in the Union Army, then to declare slaves free, and to support equal suffrage. The Civil War was now a crusade for freedom, and they felt there was no freedom without the vote.

A petition for the right to vote by a group of New Orleans Blacks was sent to the President Lincoln and to Congress on March 13, 1864. It bore a thousand signatures. Twenty-seven of the signers were Andrew Jackson's

Another day dawned and love's labor commenced in earnest. Doors were opened, and rooms ventilated: bed-clothing aired and sunned, and dusting brushes and brooms in willing hands removed every particle of that much dreaded material of which man in all his glory, or ignominy, was created. Furniture and picture frames were polished and artistically arranged. And we beheld the work of the first day, and it was good.

When another day dawned we were up with the lark, and his matin notes found responsive melody in our hearts, the sweet refrain of which was, "Thomie is coming" — the soldier son and brother. Light bread and rolls, rusks and pies, cakes, etc., etc., were baked, and sweetmeats prepared, and another day's work was ended and pronounced satisfactory.

The third day, for a generous bonus, "Uncle Mack's" services were secured, and a fine pig was slaughtered and prepared for the oven, and also a couple of young hens, and many other luxuries too numerous to mention.

When all was ready for the feast of thanksgiving for the return of the loved one, the waiting seemed interminable. There was pathos in every look, tone, and act of our mother — the lingering look at the calendar, the frequent glance at the clock, told that the days were counted, yea, that the hours were numbered. At length the weary waiting ended, and the joyous meeting came of mother and son, of sisters and brother, after a separation of four years of health and sickness, of joy and anguish, of hope and fear.

As we stood upon the platform of the Decatur depot, and saw him step from the train, which we had been told by telegram would bring him to us, our hearts were filled with consternation and pity, and tears unbidden coursed down our cheeks, as we looked upon the brave and gallant brother, who had now given three years of his early manhood to a cause rendered by inheritance and the highest principles of patriotism, and, in doing so, had himself become a physical wreck. He was lean to emaciation, and in his pale face was not a suggestion of the ruddy color he had carried away. A constant cough, which he tried in vain to repress, betrayed the deep inroads which prison life had made upon his system; and in this respect he represented his friends — in describing his appearance, we leave nothing untold about theirs. In war-worn pants and faded grey coats, they presented spectacle never to be forgotten.

Joy and grief contended for the supremacy. We did not realize that even a brief period of good nursing and feeding would work a great change in the physical being of men just out of the prison pens of the frigid North, and wept to think that disease, apparently so deeply rooted, could not be cured, and that they were restored to us but to die. Perceiving our grief and divining the cause, our Thomie took us, our mother first, into his arms and kissed us, and said in his old-time way, "I'll be all right soon."

— from *Life in Dixie During the War,* by Mary A. H. Gay

## Camp life

Camp life could be slow and even relaxed compared to the action on a battlefield. The memoirs of Robert W. Patrick, published in 1886, offer this view of life in an army camp:

"In this sultry season the river that flowed by the camp was a sanitary agent of the utmost value, and it was no uncommon sight to see thousands at once bathing in the clear waters of the placid stream, disporting themselves as if the army had suddenly become amphibious, and was seeking its foe at the bottom of the flowing river.

"These exercises in the water were paralleled by as active physical exercises on the land, pitching quoits — or horse shoes. . . running, jumping, wrestling, and all possible methods of getting rid of superabundant muscular vitality.

"It must not be said, however, that all the men of the army occupied themselves in these rude physical sports. A walk around the camp at any time would reveal numbers otherwise engaged. Hundreds might be seen seated in the shadows of their tents, engaged in reading, or in studies of various kinds in accordance with their tastes and opportunities. Others seemed to spend a great portion of their time in correspondence, shedding ink as profusely as they had recently shed blood; while many others seemed satisfied with the mere enjoyment of life, lying for hours on their backs in the warm bath of the sunshine. . . ."

soldiers at the Battle of New Orleans in the War of 1812. After deliberating four days at the National Negro Convention in Syracuse, New York, in October of 1864, the 144 delegates from eighteen states drew up an "Address to the People of the United States." It claimed that Blacks had earned the right to vote and asked, "Are we citizens when the nation is in peril, and aliens when the nation is in safety? May we shed our blood under the star-spangled banner on the battlefield, and yet be barred from marching under it at the ballot-box?"

Some African-American women from the North worked in hospitals or camps. Others raised money for the families of men at the front, to buy flags and banners for regiments, or to buy food for ill and convalescent soldiers. A number of women's groups helped newly arrived former slaves, giving them food and clothing. One such group was the Contraband Relief Society, made up of forty women in Washington, D.C., who helped fugitives who had

## Andersonville and other POW horrors

A Civil War prisoner would have thought it strange — people driving proudly around today with prisoner-of-war license plates or flags asking us to remember prisoners still alive in Vietnam. How times change!

In the nineteenth century, capture alive and whole by the enemy was considered disgraceful. If a soldier was gravely wounded, he stood a poor chance of surviving and was frequently killed out of mercy by friends or by advancing enemy troops. A wounded soldier able to walk yet unable to fight was the only acceptable description of a prisoner of war. The Union's Black soldiers were hardly ever taken prisoner but were instead shot when captured. Once in a prison, soldiers faced other hardships.

To end the conflict sooner, Union General Ulysses S. Grant stopped trading prisoners with the South in the middle of the war. Why, he reasoned, should he hand back to the enemy soldiers who would try again to kill his troops? The result was overcrowding in places such as Andersonville, Georgia, a Confederate prison where thirteen thousand Union soldiers died, many of thirst, during a drought in the summer of 1864. Prisoners also died of starvation, of infection from wounds, and from disease.

The commander of the prison, Captain Henry Wirz, was hanged following a postwar trial. Pioneering nurse Clara Barton later led a campaign to mark the graves of those who died in Andersonville, the largest military prison of the Civil War.

escaped to the capital. Some groups sent money to slaves or free Blacks in the South. The Colored Ladies Sanitary Commission of Boston, for example, sent five hundred dollars to suffering free Blacks in Savannah.

## The Cost of War

In every conceivable way, the cost of war was high. Families were torn when one brother fought for the Union and another fought for the Confederacy. Even President Lincoln's family split loyalties, as Mary A. H. Gay's memoirs point out:

> The Magnolia Cadets, under the leadership of Captain N. H. R. Dawson, of Selma [Alabama], were among the first to respond [to the Confederate call to arms]. I accompanied my cousins . . . to see this company of noble, handsome young men. . . .
>
> It was a beautiful sight! Wealthy, cultured young gentlemen voluntarily turning their backs upon the luxuries and endearments of affluent homes, and accepting in lieu the privations and hardships of warfare; thereby illustrating to the world that the conflict of arms consequent upon the secession was not to be "a rich man's war and a poor man's fight."
>
> I saw them as they stood in line to receive the elegant silken banner, bearing the stars and bars of a new nation, made and presented to them by Miss Ella Todd and her sister, Mrs. Dr. White, of Lexington, Kentucky, who were introduced to the audience by Captain Dawson as the sisters of Mrs. Abraham Lincoln, the wife of the president of the United States.

The Battle of Antietam, 1862.

## Pickett's Charge — a terrible harvest

It is a cruel irony that Pickett's Charge during the Battle of Gettysburg occurred on a rolling field of ripening wheat: southern soldiers fell as if cut by a scythe. And like wheat, behind every falling stalk there seemed to be another, awaiting a terrible harvest.

Confederate troops under General Robert E. Lee went looking for new shoes in southern Pennsylvania in the summer of 1863. Instead, they found a small band of Union cavalry soon joined by reinforcements under Union General George Meade.

The climax of the awful, three-day Battle of Gettysburg came on the afternoon of July 3. Three lines of southern foot soldiers, fifteen thousand strong, marched with bayonets glistening across an open wheat field three-quarters of a mile long toward woodsy Cemetery Ridge, filled with well-armed Union troops. Many of the Confederates were killed by artillery fire, but others reached the woods under cover of smoke from exploding shells.

The Union soldiers waited until the surviving, fast-marching men in grey were within a few feet and then opened fire. For a few minutes, the line of blue bent but did not break. All of the Confederates who made it to the ridge were soon killed or captured.

Every Confederate general and all twenty regimental commanders in the battle were either killed or wounded.

General Meade's inability and General Lee's determination prevented Lee's retreating army from being caught and slaughtered. The Confederates were able to cross the Potomac River back into Virginia. Another quick confrontation in Pennsylvania might have shortened the war.

I was thus made aware that Mrs. Lincoln and her illustrious husband were Southerners. I have since been in the small, mud-chinked log cabin in Elizabethtown, Kentucky, in which he was born, and in which his infancy and little boyhood were domiciled. Mrs. White had married an Alabamian, and as his wife, became a citizen of his State. Her sister, Miss Todd, was visiting her at the enactment of the scene described, and under like circumstances, also became a citizen of Alabama. She married the valiant gentleman who introduced her to the public on that memorable occasion.

Some families never recovered from the deaths of fathers, sons, brothers, husbands, and lovers. Weeks might pass between a soldier's death and the day his family was notified. At the Battle of Gettysburg, a burial detail came upon the body of a Union soldier clutching a photo of his three children. Word of the "children of the battlefield" spread. Efforts to identify the father blossomed into a Union-wide campaign. Thousands of copies of the picture were circulated. A fifty-dollar prize was offered for the best poem about the tragedy, and the winning piece was put to music.

In November 1863, Mrs. Amos Humiston recognized the picture she had sent to her husband, a sergeant in Company C, 154th New York Infantry. Money from the sale of the photographs and the sheet music established the Soldiers' Orphans' Home in Gettysburg in 1866. Humiston's widow became the first matron of the home, and her children were educated there.

A photo taken of a Civil War hospital by official Union photographer Mathew Brady.

## The Landscape Runs Red

All battles had casualties, but the Battle of Antietam, fought near Sharpsburg, Maryland, on September 17, 1862, marked one of the bloodiest days in American history. By nightfall, witnesses reported that the landscape seemed to have turned red. Total casualties numbered more than twenty-five thousand, of whom almost five thousand were killed. Even though Antietam was not a clear-cut Union victory, at least it was not a defeat. It was successful enough that President Lincoln issued the Emancipation Proclamation, which declared the freedom of slaves within the Confederacy. After Antietam, the war thus became a war for freedom as well as a war to preserve the Union. Also, the North's apparent victory convinced European powers to remain neutral, dashing the South's hopes for foreign assistance.

This battle also had a particularly strong impact on the nation because it was the first to be documented with cameras. Photographs by New Yorker Mathew Brady showed dead soldiers and animals on the battlefield. They were displayed at Brady's studio in an exhibit called "The Dead of Antietam." Viewers were shocked — civilians saw that war was not the glamorous thing they had been led to believe.

Soldiers were not the only ones to suffer during the Civil War. Civilians in the South had to suffer not only the loss of loved ones in the military, but also the ravaging of their homes. Plantations were looted and sometimes destroyed. Women, especially Black women, were assaulted by Union soldiers. Entire cities burned. Even slave cabins were looted. One Union soldier was reprimanded by a slave woman for stealing her quilt when he was supposed to be fighting for her freedom. "You're a . . . liar," he retorted. "I'm fighting for $14 a month and the

Union." Henry D. Jenkins, an ex-slave from South Carolina, remembered the Yankees as "a army dat seemed more concerned 'bout stealin' than they was 'bout de Holy War for de liberation of de poor African slave people."

## Primitive Health Care

As great as the losses on the battlefield were during the Civil War, the losses to disease were greater. Although improvements in surgery took place during the war, some doctors were poorly informed and provided inadequate treatment to sick and wounded soldiers. Typhus, tuberculosis, food poisoning, influenza, malaria, dysentery — these and other diseases flourished wherever soldiers from different parts of the country came together. Physicians had the skills to administer anesthetics and to amputate limbs. But internal medicine was in its infancy during the early 1860s, and doctors had not yet discovered the germ theory of disease. Surgeons operated in field hospitals without washing their hands, unknowingly contributing to gangrene and other infections.

In his memoirs, veteran Benjamin Taylor describes at length one hospital in a church:

> And the churches of Chattanooga had congregations [of the wounded]. Those who composed them had come silent and suffering and of steady hearts; had come upon stretchers, come in men's arms, like infants to the christening; ambulances had been drawing up to the church-doors all night with their burdens, and within those walls it looked one great altar of sacrifice. . . . The doors are noiselessly opening and closing, and I see pale faces — bloody garments. Right hands lie in the porch that have offended and been cut off; castaway feet are there, too. . . .
>
> Five still figures, covered by five brown blankets, are ranged on the floor beside me. Their feet are manacled with bits of slender twine, but a spider's thread could hold them. I lift a corner of the blanket and look at the quiet faces. By the gray coat I see that one is a dead rebel. Do men look nearer alike when dead than when alive? Else how could it have chanced that one of these sleepers in Federal blue should resemble him nearly enough for both to have been "twinned at birth"? They are not wounded in the face, and so there is nothing to shock you; they fell in their full strength. Tread lightly, lest he be not dead, but sleeping.
>
> The silence within oppresses me; it seems as if an accent of pain from some sufferer in that solemn church would be a welcome sound, and I think of a brave bird wounded unto death, that I have held in my hand, its keen eye undimmed and full upon me, throbbing with the pain and the dying, and yet so silent.

## Freedom and Its Sobering Reality

There was no universal celebration among Blacks in the South when the Confederacy under General Robert E. Lee surrendered on April 9, 1865, in Appomattox, Virginia. While few slaves had any reservations about their desire to be free, freedom brought with it a huge sense of uncertainty and even anxiety.

An illustrated edition of the *Declaration of Independence* issued in 1861, amended to include African-Americans.

THE AMERICAN DECLARATION OF INDEPENDENCE ILLUSTRATED.

Published by THAYER & CO. Boston.

Life as they knew it in the South would never be the same. And while this meant an end to their enslavement, it also meant an unclear future and a present that surrounded them with mass poverty and destruction beyond anything they might have imagined. After the war, many southern Blacks and whites alike were refugees depending on the federal government for help. Getting started in a new life would not be easy.

Although slaves generally welcomed the sight of Yankee troops during the Civil War, the behavior and attitudes of many Union soldiers toward African-Americans were not necessarily less racist than those of Confederate soldiers.

Many former slaves were thus fearful of the future because they did not trust whites — not even northern whites — while others remained loyal to their former masters. Change, even longed-for change, is not always easy.

Throughout the Civil War, African-Americans often protected their masters when it was not in their best interests. When an armed and drunken Union soldier abused a white lady on a Columbia, South Carolina, street, two unarmed Blacks came to her aid. In another incident, Charley Williams, an ex-slave, described how Yankee troops ordered his master to dance. The master refused, but the white man's former slaves danced to protect his life.

Another ex-slave recalled taking a gun from his master and locking him in the smokehouse to prevent a suicidal confrontation with Union forces. This protection continued after the war ended. "Shorty" Wadley Clemons of Alabama, for example, could not stand by and watch his old mistress starve after her husband died and she lost her land. He was financially secure and supported her until her death. He would have paid for her funeral had not local whites decided he had done enough.

Twentieth-century historian and Black activist W. E. B. DuBois said that African-Americans "felt pity and responsibility and also a certain new undercurrent of independence." But one ex-slave, Katie Rose of Arkansas, had a more critical view. "People who say that slavery days were better, didn't have no white master and overseer lak we all had on our place. I hear my chillun read about General Lee, and I know he was a good man, but I didn't know nothing about him den, but I know he wasn't fighting for dat kind of wite folks."

Some who had suffered were able to forgive. Elizabeth Keckley, who worked as a maid for the Jefferson Davis family and later for the Lincoln family, put it this way: "Even I, who was once a slave, who have been punished with the cruel lash, who have experienced the heart and torture of a slave's life, can say to Mr. Jefferson Davis, 'Peace! You have suffered! Go in peace!'"

## Tragedy at War's End

Regardless of how African-Americans felt about the end of the war, they deeply respected President Lincoln. They had heard of his graciousness to African-Americans who showed up at the White House, whether on public occasions, such as a New Year's Day reception, or on personal visits. A delegation of Baltimore Blacks who presented him with a huge ornamented Bible found him cordial and kind. African-Americans were also heartened by Lincoln's support of the Thirteenth Amendment to the Constitution (which abolished slavery) and cheered the House of Representatives vote on January 31, 1865, giving the necessary two-thirds majority for ratification. They felt this formal acceptance of their emancipation had begun with Lincoln's remarks about "a new birth of freedom" in his Gettysburg Address on November 19, 1863. They trusted him to lead the nation through this birth of freedom with fairness and dignity.

Such hopes were dashed when Lincoln was assassinated at Ford's Theatre in Washington, D.C., by John Wilkes Booth on April 14, 1865. We can only wonder how different things might be today if Lincoln had lived to help reunite the nation.

Freed Blacks in a southern town shortly after the Civil War.

# CHAPTER FIVE

# Toward Freedom

Lincoln had great hopes for healing the wounds between North and South after the Civil War and for helping African-Americans make the transition from slavery to freedom. But his death left a huge void. Lincoln's vice president, Andrew Johnson, was now president, and as such was in charge of southern Reconstruction, as the congressional plan was known. Reconstruction was a postwar plan to maintain order, monitor relations between European-Americans and African-Americans, and help a slave's transition to freedom.

Johnson lacked Lincoln's skill and character; he was stubborn and disregarded his advisors. When his appointees and military officers addressed former slaves, now called freedmen, they forgot the role Blacks had played in the North's victory. They even told Black veterans that African-Americans were not involved in the struggle and that the war had been the white man's business. The new president's people felt equality was something Blacks must earn. Some northern officers urged freedmen to stay on the land, obey the old slaveowners, and even to continue calling their former owners "master" and "mistress."

In December 1865, former Confederate General Robert V. Richardson, treasurer of the American Cotton Planters' Association, told planters, "The emancipated slaves own nothing, because nothing but freedom has been given to them." African-Americans had been thrown upon the labor market poor, illiterate, and disadvantaged. Johnson didn't listen to voices calling for land or other kinds of compensation for Blacks, who had endured hundreds of years of oppression.

Even though freedom may not have been what ex-slaves had hoped, they understood their new status. Addressing Congress in 1883, the Reverend E. P. Holmes, a former house servant, said, "Most anyone ought to know that a man is better

General Oliver Otis
Howard.

off free than as a slave, even if he did not have anything. I would rather be free and have my liberty. I fared just as well as any white child could have fared when I was a slave, and yet I would not give up my freedom."

Another freed African-American, Margaret Nullin of Texas, said, "In slavery, I owns nothin' and never owns nothing. In freedom I's own de home and raise de family. All dat cause me worriment, and in slavery I had no worriment. But I takes de freedom."

## Freedmen at Work

Most freedmen were more than willing to exert themselves. In Memphis, for example, among more than 16,000 freedmen in June of 1865, only 220 were unable or unwilling to care for themselves, mostly because of either physical disability or old age. In response to the plight of these and other freedmen, Black benevolent societies were formed to help those who could not help themselves.

Nearly one hundred privately financed freedmen's aid societies sprung up, serving former slaves and poor whites alike. General Oliver Otis Howard was the commissioner of the federal Freedmen's Bureau, an agency of Reconstruction. He oversaw a health program that distributed 21 million medical rations, established forty hospitals, and treated nearly half a million cases of illness in the bureau's seven years of existence. In addition, the bureau helped locate and reunite family members who had been sold away from one another during slavery. It also served as legal counsel for freedmen in cases dealing with confiscated and abandoned lands. Most such land, however, was inferior and undesirable.

The Freedmen's Bureau also was responsible for establishing schools. More than four thousand schools, from elementary through college, were created by the federal authorities. The schools charged neither tuition nor fees, and textbooks were often free, too. Nearly 250,000 former slaves received at least some education in these institutions. Bureau educational officials spent more than $5 million establishing the first schools for southern Blacks.

The proportion of the bureau's African-American teachers by the mid-1870s totaled 50 to 75 percent in North Carolina and Louisiana and 35 percent in

School for freed Black
slaves.

Alabama, Georgia, and South Carolina. These teachers ranged from college-educated Blacks who had been free before the War to barely literate freedmen. Those with the best qualifications were generally employed in Mobile, Charleston, Savannah, or New Orleans, while the less educated taught in rural or plantation schools considered too backward for northern female teachers. Only Louisiana and South Caro-

A Reconstruction political cartoon mocks white resistance to the bestowing of liberty on slaves.

lina permitted racially mixed schools. South Carolina mixed races in sparsely populated areas where the cost of separate schools would have been too great.

Many Blacks stayed on or near their former farms or plantations, while others left, often to find lost relatives. Others took to the open road to confirm that they really were free. In the months immediately following the war, some waited for the promise of a mule and forty acres. Neither the animal nor the real estate was ever given these patient people.

## White Backlash

Although they had been defeated, white southerners were not eager to give up power, privilege, and domination over Blacks. Most whites still felt people of color were inferior, and the end of slavery did not mean the end of racism. They were seething about the loss of the war, they were seething about the loss of $2 billion in slave property, and they hated the fact that their way of life was in disarray.

Southern planters disliked the role of the Freedmen's Bureau as mediator between slaves and European-American landowners. They also disliked the creation of schools for African-Americans, feeling that "Blacks couldn't absorb learning." They were especially outraged at Yankee teachers fostering social equality by eating with Blacks and addressing them as "Miss" or "Mister."

Southerners fought back with legislation called Black Codes. Enacted by state legislatures in the fall and winter of 1865-66, these codes were designed to control former slaves. The codes also were passed by southern state legislatures in the interval between the end of the war in 1865 and Congress' passing in 1867 of Reconstruction legislation, which abolished the Black Codes and protected the rights of African-Americans. The code in South Carolina stated that in the making of contracts, "persons of color shall be known as servants and those with whom they contract shall be known as master." The South Carolina code stated that an African-American farm worker could not leave a job without permission and that Blacks could have no jobs other than farming or domestic service unless they paid an annual tax ranging from ten to one hundred dollars.

Two northern legislators who represented antislavery interests in Washington, D.C.: Thaddeus Stevens (top) and Charles Sumner (bottom).

Vagrancy laws were enacted to further subdue the African-American population. In Mississippi, for example, vagrancy laws were applied only to unemployed Blacks. If victims of the law did not pay the fine, they were hired out by the sheriff. Mississippi vagrancy statutes covered "rogues and vagabonds, idle and dissipated persons, beggars, jugglers, or persons practicing unlawful games or plays, runaways, common drunkards . . . common railers and brawlers, persons who neglect their calling or employment, misspend what they earn, or do not provide for the support of themselves or their families, or dependents, and all other idle and disorderly persons, including all who neglect all lawful business, habitually misspend their time by frequenting . . . gaming houses, or tippling shops."

Local ordinances in Louisiana required that every Black be in the service of some white or of a former owner who was responsible for his or her conduct. The codes usually forbade African-Americans to join the militia or to own firearms. A special license to preach might even be required.

Policies meant to keep Blacks as second-class citizens, called "Jim Crow" rules, were part of the post-war picture, too. These laws, which were first established in Tennessee in 1875, differed from the Black Codes primarily in that they had one principal aim: to separate the races. Mississippi African-Americans were forbidden to ride among European-Americans in first-class passenger cars. A Florida Black man could be given thirty-nine lashes for "intruding himself into any religious or other assembly of white persons." Blacks couldn't vote and sometimes weren't allowed to testify in court against whites.

African-Americans did have the right to own property, to sue each other, to testify in court in cases involving Blacks, and to have legal marriages. But except for the efforts of the Freedmen's Bureau, they were virtually without protection. Blacks were in some ways even more at the mercy of whites than they had been under the slave laws, where as "property" they at least had the protection of their owner. Now that whites no longer owned other human beings, postwar law became a means of enforcing white property rights against their former slaves.

Taxes also became a way of maintaining white power. Taxes on land were extremely low (one-tenth of one percent in Mississippi, for example). But freedmen faced high poll taxes if they tried to vote, and the earnings of urban craftspeople were taxed. Many Blacks who received land during Reconstruction lost it at tax sales, where land was auctioned to the highest bidder because the owner had failed to pay taxes promptly.

## Northern Outrage and Action

These codes and taxes enraged most northerners, who saw this as slavery with a new name. Many northerners came to believe that intervention by the federal government was necessary if Black rights were to be protected. This feeling lent political support to the Republicans, who did not want to see the white aristocracy regain power in the South. The Republicans wanted African-Americans to retain their newly gained rights. At the same time, northern industrialist interests wanted to be sure that they had access to the southern economy—a goal that would never be realized if the South were allowed to return to an agriculturally-based economic system. Northerners were also worried that such a system would create the same labor needs that had allowed slavery to flourish in the South.

This combination of political, civil-rights, and economic interests resulted in a stern attitude toward the South from the federal government. Congress refused immediate readmission of the southern states to the Union, claiming that conditions in the South had to be studied, and the Republicans appointed a Joint Committee on Reconstruction, which gathered months of testimony. The committee was headed by radical Republicans Charles Sumner of Massachusetts (representing the most abolition-minded state) and Thaddeus Stevens (a Pennsylvanian who was familiar with Quaker sentiments against slavery). Meanwhile, in April 1866, Congress passed a civil rights act extending citizenship to former slaves. The act noted that discrimination against former slaves would be tried in federal courts rather than state courts. This act had the effect not only of promoting African-American civil rights, but also of strengthening the hand of the federal govern-

*Top:* A political cartoon portraying the so-called freedom of the African-American voter.
*Bottom:* Blacks voting in Richmond during Reconstruction, 1871.

ment in its dealings with southern states. In addition, the Fourteenth Amendment to the Constitution was passed, which guaranteed U.S. citizenship to all persons born in the United States. It said that no state could withhold the rights of its citizens or deprive any citizen of equal protection under the law. If a state withheld the ballot from any adult, its seats in the House of Representatives would suffer proportionate reduction.

Southern states would not ratify the Fourteenth Amendment, causing even more northerners to join the Republican party. The federal Reconstruction Act of March 2, 1867, called for the South to be administered by five military districts under a major general. To be readmitted to the Union, a southern state had to give Black men the vote and accept the Fourteenth Amendment. Loyal Leagues were formed in the South to attract Republican support. Their passwords were "Lincoln, liberty, loyal, league."

For a while, things looked up for African-Americans. New constitutions were drafted in southern states establishing statewide systems of free education and abolishing cruel punishments that could be used against poor people of all races, such as imprisonment for debt. Punishments such as branding, whipping, and the stocks became illegal. States passed militia laws, and many Blacks joined up. The Fifteenth Amendment, passed in 1870, stated that a citizen's right to vote should not be denied because of race or color.

African-Americans across the country held ratification ceremonies. In Baltimore, twenty thousand Blacks marched in celebration through downtown streets. Frederick Douglass, addressing the marchers, declared, "We have a future, everything is possible to us." But the tide was about to turn against the freedmen, and it would not be stemmed for many years.

There were at the time many Blacks in government. Twenty-two African-American congressmen were sent to Washington from eight southern states in the late 1860s and early 1870s. Two served in the Senate, twenty in the House of Representatives. Thirteen of the congressmen had been born in slavery, while ten were college trained, including five with college degrees. But their tenure was to be short-lived and would not outlive Reconstruction itself, which died out in the late 1870s.

In the South, African-Americans also were involved in Reconstruction government, but they weren't in control. The total membership in the southern constitutional conventions (held by individual states prior to readmission to the Union) was 713 whites, compared to 260 Blacks. Despite their large numbers, Blacks never controlled — or held significant power — in a state legislature. Yet they helped pass social legislation that benefited both Blacks and whites, and many African-American politicians became well known. In South Carolina, Jonathan J. Wright served for nearly six years as associate justice of the state supreme court. In Louisiana, William G. Brown was superintendent of education. And in Florida, Jonathan C. Gibbs was secretary of state and superintendent of instruction. Others held posts such as prosecuting attorney, superintendent of the poor, sheriff, and mayor. Most held office only at the local level, serving as justices of the peace, for example.

## Southern Resistance Grows

Despite the lack of opportunity for decision making in their former lives, many Blacks served with distinction. On the whole, though, corruption and inefficiency marked Reconstruction government. African-Americans who had never seen anything but plantation life sometimes were put in charge of complex food distribution networks and other

A carpetbagger from the North discusses politics with poor southern whites and Blacks from high on his horse.

## Reconstruction's end

Did the North end Reconstruction out of hatred or lack of concern for the South? If only the answer were a simple yes or no. . . .

The end of Reconstruction began with the 1876 Presidential election, which was too close to call. Samuel J. Tilden, a Democrat, received more popular votes than Republican Rutherford B. Hayes. But there was a disagreement over twenty-two electoral college votes, and the matter was handed to Congress. In February 1877 — a month after the usual January 20 inauguration date — Hayes was awarded the nation's highest office. In exchange, he promised southern congressmen he would end Reconstruction. It should be remembered that Tilden, with strong southern support, also would have ended Reconstruction if he had been named President.

There were other reasons for the idealistic program to end. First, Americans were by 1877 more interested in devoting federal troops and federal attention to taming the West. Custer and his 7th Cavalry troops died in 1876 at the Battle of Little Big Horn. This stunning Indian victory told northern and southern Americans alike that American Indians wouldn't settle for whatever they were to be given. Second, the late nineteenth century was a time of incredible industrialization, with plenty of opportunities to make fortunes, North or South. Third, the waves of immigrants meant more money and attention had to be paid to the cities on both coasts. Fourth, the economy rollercoastered into a deep recession in the early 1870s.

Federal authorities also worried about the rise of labor unions. Railway workers staged their first nationwide strike in 1877, paralyzing the nation's ability to move goods. That same year, eleven militant Irish miners in Pennsylvania, known as the Molly Maguires, were hanged. They were part of a new wave of European socialists and anarchists, and their willingness to use violence to make their point sent chills up the spines of politicians everywhere.

Finally, 1877 marked the twelfth year since the end of the conflict the South still calls the War Between the States. A new generation was growing up without personal knowledge of the many battles and huge losses. Those who continued to bring up the war — Black or white — were looked on by young people as living in the past.

A carpetbagger portrayed with a bag in front of him filled with others' faults, which he always sees, and a bag behind him filled with his own faults, which he never sees.

Confederate Major General Nathan B. Forrest, head of the Ku Klux Klan during Reconstruction.

bureaucratic schemes. White northern businessmen, considered opportunists by southerners but in reality part of a growing middle class, were called carpetbaggers because they showed up with their belongings in suitcases made from carpeting. They were resented because they had money and were seen as taking advantage of an economically wounded South. Even more disliked were scalawags, southern-born European-American Republicans who were looked upon as traitors by the southern, Democrat majority.

Despite the inadequacies of Reconstructionist government, however, it was in fact no more corrupt than pre-Civil War state governments in the South. Many historians argue that white southern opposition to Reconstruction was not so much based on the objection to corruption and incompetence as it was caused by the unyielding racism of southern whites and their unwillingness to give up slavery and their domination over African-Americans.

In response to their need to regain power over Blacks, many southerners, especially veterans, turned to secret societies such as the White League of Louisiana, using scare tactics to "keep Blacks in their place." The most powerful such group was the infamous Ku Klux Klan, which began in 1865 in Pulaski, Tennessee. By the spring of 1867, it was well organized and cut across state lines.

Klan members, wearing black robes emblazoned with blood-red crosses and with white circles around their eyes, frightened freedmen attempting to exercise their rights. If threats weren't enough, the Klan burned homes or turned to whippings, tar-and-featherings, or lynchings. Not only freedmen but white Republicans and whites who fraternized with Blacks were attacked. Nathan B. Forrest, head of the Klan, became so alarmed at the recklessness of local dens that he ordered the organization to disband in 1869. He was ignored.

By 1877, conservative Democrats had regained control in the South. The minute they were in office, they revised Reconstruction constitutions, removing equal rights guarantees. They held elections in secret places and they arrested Blacks the day before an election, releasing them the day after. They also stuffed ballot boxes to alter election returns.

## The North Turns Its Back

This time, there was little outrage from the North. By the mid-1870s, civil rights leaders Sumner and Stevens were dead, and northern industrialists favored a hands-off policy, partly because they wanted to open markets in the South. Once Rutherford B. Hayes was elected president in 1876, he withdrew federal troops from the South in exchange for the political support that had helped elect him.

A handful of African-Americans received government appointments. Frederick Douglass was named marshal of Washington, D.C., a post that was largely ceremonial. John Mercer Langston was named the minister to Haiti, and former Congressmen Blanche K. Bruce and Robert B. Elliott were given jobs in the Treasury Department. Most Blacks, however, had no such opportunities as the Supreme Court began to interpret the Fourteenth and Fifteenth Amendments in ways that weakened their protection.

Most northerners, even many former Abolitionists, were busy dealing with huge social changes. Problems swept under the rug during the Civil War could no longer be ignored. In Texas, for example, a huge territory between the Nueces and the Rio Grande rivers had seen tremendous friction between Anglos and Latinos. Eighty percent of all Latinos in Texas lived in this neglected area.

## The Ku Klux Klan — born to hate

Today, the Ku Klux Klan stands for all that has endured of the divisiveness and racial hatred from the era of the Civil War and Reconstruction. In the years following its origins in 1865, the Klan existed as a kind of social club — a fraternity devoted to encouraging feelings of white supremacy among southerners who were unhappy with the results of the Civil War. By 1867, it had developed into a vigilante organization whose terrorist tactics placed it beyond the control of its founders. For all practical purposes, no one person controlled the Klan as a whole, and while its charter outlined a highly organized structure, local groups quickly took charge of their own affairs.

The Klan's members were extremely hostile to Blacks, and most of its early victims were Black. But in the Reconstructionist South, the Republican Party was still very much the party of the North, and so the Klan was also violently opposed to Republican officeholders who supported the voting rights of African-Americans, as well as to whites who taught at schools for African-Americans.

One terrorist tactic of KKK night riders (shown here making an unwelcome visit to a Black family) was to recite a list of the "offenses" committed by their victims. The most common "crimes" were voting for Republicans or joining the Union League. (The Union League, also known as the Loyal League, began as a patriotic society in the North during the Civil War. After the war, it put down roots in the South as well and appealed primarily to Blacks as a social organization and a branch of the Republican Party that organized voters and urged African-Americans to stand up for their new rights.)

By 1870, the actions of the Klan had become so violent that the U.S. government finally stepped in and prosecuted some of the worse crimes. But the political scene was changing during the days of Reconstruction, and people were tiring of the issues that had so driven the Union during the Civil War. By 1873, the prosecution of the Klan had ended, thanks to half-hearted efforts in some cases and seriously understaffed prosecution offices in others.

The prosecutions did not put the Klan out of business, but its activities were greatly suppressed and to some extent driven further underground. In 1915, the Klan went through a rebirth, resurrected by the sons of people who had participated in its earlier version. It presented itself as an organization of "super-patriots" during World War I and enjoyed a national resurgence in the 1920s, when its hate list expanded to include Catholics, Jews, immigrants, political radicals, and organized labor. The Klan activities died down again at the end of the 1920s and then reignited in response to the Civil Rights Movement of the 1950s and 1960s. Today, it is still in evidence, although in relatively small numbers, not just in the rural South but throughout the U.S. in cities and suburbs as well. Klan members often team up with neo-Nazi organizations and other white-supremacist groups that purport to further Christian and patriotic goals. While the Klan has in some ways made itself more visible, it has also brought its enemies out into the open, and it is not uncommon for members of various groups opposed to the Klan's views to confront them openly, vocally, and sometimes violently in public.

**Railroad building on the Great Plains.**

Lawmen assigned to the area considered it a death sentence. Great herds of cattle roamed wild in the brush country, and rustlers crossed and recrossed the U.S.-Mexican border as cattle stealing became big business. This region — and other locales — proved that the West did indeed remain wild.

The doctrine of Manifest Destiny, proclaimed by journalist John Louis O'Sullivan in the *New York Morning News* in 1845, was put into practice with a vengeance. O'Sullivan believed America's "manifest destiny" was a God-given right to virtually all land to the Pacific — "to overspread and to possess the whole of the continent which Providence has given us for the development of the great experiment of liberty and federated self-government entrusted to us." Homesteaders, gold diggers, cowhands, and storekeepers flocked to California, Montana, Oklahoma, and Oregon. Railroads sped the process. Completed in 1869, the Transcontinental Railroad was built by Chinese laborers who laid rails from the West and by Irish laborers who laid rails from the East. This caused more strife with American Indians, who continued to be pushed off their lands.

Immigrants poured into cities on both coasts, greatly increasing population and pressure on land use and on government services. English immigrants continued to arrive. They joined Protestants from Scotland and Wales and Irish Presbyterians from Ulster to form churches that served as centers for worship and as social centers.

Some of these Anglo-Saxon immigrants fared well in the new country, others not so well. In rural areas of New York and New Jersey, and throughout Appalachia, many had little more than their pride. In her diary, Mary Chesnut uses uncomplimentary terms to describe the life of these poor rural whites, whom she calls "country crackers," many of them her third or fourth cousins: "There are Sandhillers born and Sandhillers who have fallen to that estate. Old Mrs. Simons,

## Manifest Destiny, American Indians, and the clash of cultures

The difference in cultural outlook between American Indians and European-Americans was just as strange to the Indian tribes in North America as it was to the first European immigrants who explored and settled there. Yet Indians believed in the beginning that the the two cultures could live in peace and friendship. Sadly, their hopes were misplaced.

Europeans practiced a different religion, had different family and social customs, and believed in private ownership of land and property. Indians were certainly curious about their strange European customs, yet they did not hesitate to show the newcomers how to stay alive in the wilderness. They willingly acted as interpreters and guides and accepted into their families the white men who chose to marry Indian women — even when white society turned them away.

As long as the number of European immigrants remained small, Indians and whites lived in comparative peace. But more and more immigrants started pushing westward to take over the very lands on which the Indians lived.

Perhaps the greatest difference between American Indian and European-American cultures was in the way they viewed the land. Immigrants cleared the forests, slaughtered the game, greedily mined all the gold and silver they could find, and treated the land itself as a commodity to be owned, fenced in, and built upon. Indians generally thought of themselves as custodians of the land they lived on. The earth to them was sacred, and they all shared the responsibility for maintaining it. The Indians were often horrified at what they saw as destruction and waste. At the same time, they were aware that the immigrants considered themselves superior to Indians because of their European technology and ambition for wealth.

All the Indians asked for, again and again, was to be left to live in peace and to be *respected* for their cultural differences, not hated for them. But as the immigrants began to expand westward, they justified their takeover of ancestral tribal lands with what they called the "right to discovery." In fact, in 1823, the United States Supreme Court upheld the ruling that "discovery gave exclusive title to those who made it." And when immigrants couldn't take possession by right of discovery, they took it at gunpoint.

By the mid-nineteenth century, most European-Americans believed it was God's will that they take over and rule the entire North American continent. To American Indians, this concept of "manifest destiny" meant that there was now no hope of saving their lands and very little hope of saving their tribal cultures.

Young boys working in a Pennsylvania coal mine.

now; Mr. Chesnut says she was a lady once. They are very good to her. She pays no rent for her house and the fields around it. She knits gloves, which are always bought for her sake. She has many children, all grown and gone, only one son left and he is a cripple. Once a year he has a drive in a carriage. Some uneasy candidate is sure to drive by there and haul the lame man to the polls."

And while many Anglos owned factories, mines, and railroads, many more labored. Letters from Scottish immigrants published in the *Glasgow Sentinel* give an idea of what it was like to work in America's mines: "On the days we were working we started at seven o'clock in the morning. We take breakfast before we leave home. I would like to see you sitting down before six in the morning to eat potatoes, beef, bread and butter, pies, and all kinds of fancy meats.... All the men above and below, work 10 hours. The truth is, John, when the work is brisk every miner in the place works as long and as hard as he can — digging and drawing coals all day.... But this only when the work is running brisk 5 or 6 months in the winter; and if you be fortunate ... you can make over 100 dollars a month; and 40 dollars, I am informed, can keep a very large family. Then, in the summer time they go half-time; they average about 60 dollars per month...."

Immigrants poured in from Germany, Italy, Russia, Spain, Portugal, Greece, and China. They sought work, competing with each other for employment. Blacks were not the only people who felt the sting of prejudice, as this letter from a German immigrant to an immigration official shows: "I want to congratulate your noble lawful stand you are taken in regards to undesirable immigration ... especially in keeping out they dirty low bread [sic] Jewish and Slavic element, those that live on hogs food and therefore work for a pittance. You wish you would be more stricter yet, as we have too much of this undesirable trash already. Let the nations that created them, take care of them...."

The struggle to survive was fierce, according to one Lithuanian immigrant: "When I looked away I could see on one side some big fields full of holes, and these

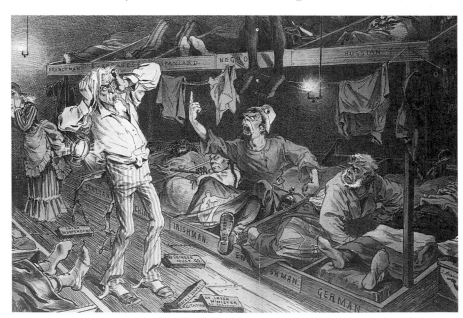

A political cartoon about immigration shows Uncle Sam criticizing the Irish for "all the time a-kicking up a row" when "everybody else is quiet and peaceable."

were the city dumps. On the other side were the stockyards, with twenty tall slaughterhouse chimneys. The wind blew a big smell from them to us. Then we walked on between the yards and the dumps and all the houses looked bad and poor. In our house my room was in the basement. I lay down on the floor with three other men and the air was rotten. I did not go to sleep for a long time. I knew then that money was everything I needed. My money was almost gone and I thought that I would soon die unless I got a job, for this was not like home. Here money was everything and a man without money must die."

A Chinese immigrant to California tells a different story. He worked and saved enough money in two years to start a laundry for men employed by the railroad, some five hundred miles inland: "A man got me work as a house servant in an American family. . . . I did not know how to do anything, and I did not understand what the lady said to me, but she showed me how to cook,

Anti-Chinese riots in Denver, 1880.

wash, iron, sweep, dust, make beds, wash dishes, clean windows, paint and brass, polish the knives and forks, etc., by doing the things herself and then overseeing my efforts to imitate her. She would take my hands and show them how to do things. She and her husband and children laughed at me a great deal, but it was all good natured. . . ."

A Japanese woman on the West Coast described her work in this way: "At noon I had to prepare a meal for twelve. The employees worked from 8:00 A.M. to 5:00 P.M., but I began to fix the dinner at 5:00 P.M., cooking for five or six persons, and then after that I started my night work. The difficult ironing and pressing was left for me. At that time ladies' blouses were high-necked and long-sleeved, with much silk lace and other decoration. I could barely iron two blouses an hour, taking great pains to press out each scallop with the point of the iron. Frequently I had to work till twelve or one o'clock."

## Entering an Era of Indifference

With so much frantic activity, northerners ignored the plight of southern Blacks as Reconstruction came to a bitter and disappointing end in 1877. Freedmen found it more difficult to vote. By 1890, would-be voters in Mississippi had to pay a poll tax and demonstrate an ability to read or interpret a section of the state

Rosa Parks and the late civil rights leader Dr. Martin Luther King at a 1965 dinner in a previously segregated Birmingham, Alabama, hotel.

constitution. By 1895, South Carolina did the same, adding a list of crimes that took away the right to vote.

Without the protection of the Freedmen's Bureau, many Blacks could only be share tenants (if they were fortunate) or sharecroppers, often on the plantations or farms where they had been slaves. Share tenants were given their own livestock and farming utensils and got a portion of the crop produced. Sharecroppers furnished only their own labor and needed credit for everything — work animals, tools, fertilizer, food for livestock, cabins, plus rations of hogback, cornmeal, and molasses. Sharecroppers received smaller portions of the crop for their work and often ended up deeply in debt.

Robbed of political power, abandoned by northern supporters, and struggling for survival, African-Americans looked to their churches for inspiration. Black clergymen became leaders because they were not dependent upon the good will of the European-American community. They could speak frankly to and for their congregations. The African-American church became a community center for recreation and relaxation, a welfare agency, a comfort to the sick and poor, and a training ground in self-government, handling of money, and management. African-American churches also started schools for the purpose of giving children a Christian education. By 1900, African-American Baptists were supporting eighty elementary and high schools. It is not surprising that leaders like Dr. Martin Luther King, Jr., and the Reverend Jesse Jackson came from the clergy.

Blacks struggled against the tide of prejudice, economic disadvantage, and political disenfranchisement that engulfed them after Reconstruction. Not until Rosa Parks refused to move to the back of a southern bus in 1955, and the sit-ins, protests, and legal cases of the 1960s, would the Emancipation

With fists clenched and heads bowed, U.S. athletes Tom Smith and John Carlos give the Black Power salute during the playing of the U.S. National Anthem at the Olympic medal awards ceremonies in Mexico City, 1968. Their silent gesture was one of both Black pride and defiance toward a society that could parade the accomplishments of African-Americans before the world while tolerating racial injustice at home.

Proclamation begin to be fulfilled. Many people today live each day according to a legacy of racial injustice and disadvantage imposed by centuries of slavery and the half-hearted transition to freedom during and after Reconstruction. There is no living person in the U.S. today whose life has not been influenced by the Civil War and, in its aftermath, the broken promise of Reconstruction.

| | |
|---|---|
| 1619 | The first African laborers, termed indentured servants, are brought to Jamestown, Virginia |
| 1650 | Slavery is legalized in the American colonies |
| 1712 | Slaves revolt in New York City; leaders of the revolt are either executed or driven to commit suicide |
| 1741 | A second revolt by slaves in New York City results in thirteen slaves hanged, thirteen burned, and seventy-one deported |
| 1774 | Rhode Island is the first colony to abolish slavery |
| 1783 | The Massachusetts Supreme Court outlaws slavery |
| 1784 | Thomas Jefferson's proposal to ban slavery in new U.S. territories after 1802 is narrowly defeated |
| 1787 | The U.S. Constitution is adopted by delegates meeting in Philadelphia on Sept. 17 |
| 1793 | Eli Whitney invents the cotton gin |
| 1808 | Slave importation is outlawed |
| 1820 | The first organized immigration of Blacks to Africa from the U.S. sails for Sierra Leone in February; Henry Clay's Missouri Compromise allows Missouri to be a slave state but prohibits slavery elsewhere west of there and north of the midwestern state's southern border |
| 1831 | William Lloyd Garrison begins his abolitionist newspaper, *The Liberator*, Jan. 1; Nat Turner and followers kill fifty-seven white people before the slave rebellion is stopped; Turner is eventually caught, tried, and hanged |
| 1835 | Oberlin College in Ohio refuses to bar students on the basis of race |
| 1852 | Harriet Beecher Stowe's *Uncle Tom's Cabin* is published |
| 1854 | The Republican Party is founded in Ripon, Wisconsin |
| 1856 | Lawrence, Kansas, is sacked by pro-slavery whites; abolitionist John Brown and party attack a Missouri town |
| 1857 | The U.S. Supreme Court rules in the Dred Scott decision that a slave is still a slave in free territory, that Congress cannot bar slavery from a territory, and that African-Americans cannot be citizens |
| 1859 | John Brown and friends seize the U.S. Armory at Harper's Ferry, West Virginia; U.S. Marines retake the facility; Brown is convicted of treason and hanged |
| 1860 | Abraham Lincoln is elected President; South Carolina secedes from the Union in December |
| 1861 | Mississippi, Alabama, Florida, Georgia, Louisiana, and Texas join South Carolina to form the Confederate States of America on Feb. 8, with Jefferson Davis of Mississippi as President; Virginia, Tennessee, Arkansas, and North Carolina eventually fill out the eleven-state C.S.A.; the Civil War begins on April 12 as Confederate forces fire on Ft. Sumter, South Carolina; President Lincoln calls up 75,000 for three months of military service; Confederates turn back Union forces at the first Battle of Bull Run, Virginia, July 21 |
| 1862 | Union forces capture New Orleans and find success in western battles |
| 1863 | President Lincoln issues the Emancipation Proclamation, freeing all slaves, Jan. 1; "The high water mark of the Confederacy" is established at tiny Gettysburg, Pennsylvania, when Union troops turn back General Robert E. Lee and his army, July 1-4. Some 51,000 soldiers on both sides die in the war's bloodiest battle |

| 1864 | Ulysses S. Grant is named commander of the Union Army, March 10; General Sherman marches through Georgia, capturing Atlanta on Sept. 1 |
| --- | --- |
| 1865 | Robert E. Lee surrenders 27,800 Confederate troops to Ulysses S. Grant at Appomatox, Virginia, on April 9, ending the war; an actor with southern sympathies, John Wilkes Booth, shoots President Lincoln in Washington's Ford's Theatre, April 14; Lincoln dies the following day; the Thirteenth Amendment, abolishing slavery, goes into effect Dec. 18 |
| 1866 | The Ku Klux Klan is founded in Pulaski, Tennessee, to terrorize Blacks who attempt to vote; Congress takes control of Reconstruction, backing the rights of freed Blacks |
| 1872 | The Amnesty Act restores rights to those who fought for the Confederacy, except for five hundred of its leaders |
| 1875 | The Civil Rights Act is passed, giving African-Americans equal rights in public accommodation and permitting them to serve as jurors |
| 1876 | Rutherford B. Hayes wins the Presidency after Republicans obtain several Electoral College votes by pledging to end federal Reconstruction. |

## GLOSSARY

| abolish | to do away with |
| --- | --- |
| abolition | in the 1700s and 1800s, doing away with slavery; abolitionists actively opposed slavery and worked for its demise |
| anarchist | a person who believes that all forms of government or authority are oppressive and undesirable and should be abolished; some but not all anarchists use active resistance and terrorism against the government to promote their cause |
| belligerent | hostile, aggressive, or eager to fight |
| Electoral College | a body of voters who are chosen in presidential elections to cast the actual votes for president and vice president of the U.S.; when U.S. citizens cast ballots for presidential candidates of their choice, they are actually voting for the members of the Electoral College who have indicated their commitment to that candidate |
| immigrant | a person who comes into a foreign country to live |
| Industrial Revolution | major social and economic changes that come about when systems of producing goods shift from home-based hand manufacturing to large-scale factory production; the Industrial Revolution in Europe and North America in the 1800s resulted in increased use of machinery and created an entirely different labor force from that which had existed before |
| Ku Klux Klan | a secret society formed in the South to prevent African-Americans from exercising their rights; in time it expanded its hate list to include Jews, Catholics, and immigrants |
| persecution | the act of oppressing or harassing someone, usually on the basis of race, ethnic background, gender, religion, sexual orientation, or beliefs that differ from those of the persecutor |
| plantation | a large farm or estate where work is done by slave laborers who live there |
| poll tax | a tax used as a prerequisite for voting; often used to prevent Blacks from exercising their right to vote |

| | |
|---|---|
| **race bait** | to persistently attack, torment, or ridicule someone on the basis of that person's racial or ethnic heritage |
| **Reconstruction** | period after the Civil War when southern states were reorganized and brought back into the Union |
| **repatriation** | returning people to their native lands |
| **secession** | formally withdrawing from an organization or nation |
| **socialist** | someone who believes in a social system in which political power is exercised by the entire community and the means of producing and distributing goods is owned and controlled by the community |
| **territory** | land belonging to a government; in the U.S. and Canada, territories are lands that are owned by the government, and whose residents enjoy certain rights and privileges of U.S. or Canadian citizenship, but that are not U.S. states or Canadian provinces |
| **Ulster** | a historical region and ancient kingdom of Ireland; it is often used as the term to describe the territory of northern Ireland that is now a part of the United Kingdom (Britain) known as Northern Ireland |
| **Underground Railroad** | network of slaves, free Blacks, and antislavery whites that secretly moved escapees from the South to free states in the North or to Canada |
| **vigilance committees** | groups founded by free Blacks to help runaway slaves |

## FURTHER READING

Beatty, Patricia. *Turn Homeward, Hannalee*. Mahwah: Troll Associates, 1984.

Beatty, Patricia. *Charley Skedaddle*. Mahwah: Troll Associates, 1987.

Davidson, Margaret. *Frederick Douglass Fights For Freedom*. New York: Scholastic, Inc., 1968.

Davis, Kenneth C. *Don't Know Much About History*. New York: Avon Books, 1990.

Ferris, Jerri. *Go Free or Die*. Minneapolis: Carolrhoda Books, Inc., 1988.

Franklin, John Hope. *From Slavery to Freedom*. New York: Knopf. Sixth edition, 1988.

Fritz, Jean. *Stonewall*. New York: Puffin Books, 1979.

Hansen, Joyce. *Which Way Freedom*. New York: Avon Books, 1986.

Hoobler, Dorothy and Hoobler, Thomas. *Next Stop, Freedom*. Englewood Cliffs: Silver Burdett Press, Inc., 1991.

McMullan, Kate. *The Story of Harriet Tubman, Conductor of the Underground Railroad*. New York: Dell Publishing, 1991.

Myers, Walter Dean. *Now Is Your Time!* New York: HarperCollins Publishers, 1991.

Rappaport, Doreen. *Escape From Slavery*. New York: HarperCollins Publishers, 1991.

Sterling, Dorothy. *Freedom Train*. New York: Scholastic, Inc., 1954.

White, Deborah Gray. *Ar'n't I a Woman?: Female Slaves in the Plantation South*. New York: W. W. Norton, 1985.

Zinn, Howard. *A People's History of the United States*. New York: Harper & Row, Publishers, 1980.

PIGGINS, CAROL ANN

A MULTICULTURAL PORTRAIT OF
THE CIVIL WAR

DEMCO